D1741944

JUGS

JUGS

Steve Quirk

NEW HOLLAND

First published in Australia in 2011 by
New Holland Publishers (Australia) Pty Ltd
Sydney • Auckland • London • Cape Town

www.newholland.com.au

1/66 Gibbes Street Chatswood NSW 2067 Australia
218 Lake Road Northcote Auckland New Zealand
86 Edgware Road London W2 2EA United Kingdom
80 McKenzie Street Cape Town 8001 South Africa

Copyright © 2011 in text: Steve Quirk
Copyright © 2011 in images: Celeste Vlok and New Holland
Image Library (page 229)
Copyright © 2011 New Holland Publishers (Australia) Pty Ltd

All rights reserved. No part of this publication may be
reproduced, stored in a retrieval system or transmitted, in any
form or by any means, electronic, mechanical, photocopying,
recording or otherwise, without the
prior written permission of the publishers and
copyright holders.

National Library of Australia Cataloguing-in-Publication details:
    Quirk, Steve, 1971-
    Jugs / Steve Quirk.

    9781742571805 (hbk,)
    Includes index.
    Punches (Beverages)/Beverages/
    Entertaining/Parties.

    641.874

Publisher: Fiona Schultz
Publishing manager: Lliane Clarke
Project editor and propping: Jodi De Vantier
Design, styling and photography: Celeste Vlok
Bartender for photoshoot: Steve Quirk
Production manager: Olga Dementiev
Printer: Everbest Printing Co. Ltd, China

Follow New Holland Publishers on Facebook:
www.facebook.com/NewHollandPublishers
and Twitter: @NewHollandAU

CONTENTS

INTRODUCTION

From basic mixers through to exotic creations, there is nothing complicated about preparing and constructing jugs and punches, as you will soon discover. Each recipe provides clear and uncomplicated directions, ensuring that even those with no experience will soon be mixing drinks with ease. Want to know how to chill a glass? How to layer ingredients? What bar equipment is required? All the answers you need are provided here, along with other useful tips for creating perfect punches and mixed drinks.

An approximate percentage of alcohol per volume (% alc/vol) content has been supplied for each alcoholic drink recipe, as well as how many standard drinks each contains. These calculations are based on information believed to be accurate and reliable, although cannot be guaranteed due to the alcohol/volume variations between the different brands of spirits and liqueurs. These calculations should be used only as a guide. The percentage of alcohol for all spirits and liqueurs required for drinks contained within this book are provided in the glossary.

A NOTE ON MEASURES

1 dash	1ml
1 teaspoon	5g/5ml
1 tablespoon	15g/20ml
	Note: (Note: Imperial and NZ tablespoon is 15ml)
1 cup (liquid measures)	250ml (9fl oz)
Solid measures (vary, depending on substance)	
1 cup caster sugar	220g (8oz)

Total liquid amounts given for each recipe are approximates only.

HOW TO CONSTRUCT YOUR DRINKS

LAYERING

Layering a drink creates a great effect in the jug. Pour each ingredient over the back of a large spoon into your chosen jug, bowl or glass. This will allow the liquid to flow down the inside rim of the glass, creating a layering effect. Usually, the heavier ingredients are poured first.

BLENDING

When a blender is required, use only cracked or crushed ice in suitable blenders and blend until ingredients are evenly mixed.

USEFUL TIPS

FROSTING

Frosting a glass adds a new dimension to whatever you are drinking. And it looks great too. You create a frosting by coating the rim of a glass with salt or sugar. First, moisten the rim of a glass using a slice of lemon or orange. Next, hold the chosen glass by its base or stem upside down and rest gently on a flat plate containing salt or caster sugar and twist slightly. If you press down too hard on the glass, you may end up with chunks of salt or sugar sticking to the rim. Lemon is used for salt frosted rims and orange for sugar-frosted rims unless otherwise stated.

SUGAR SYRUP

To make sugar syrup, bring one cup of ordinary white sugar with one cup of water almost to the boil in a small saucepan, stirring continuously. Simmer until sugar is completely dissolved. Remove from heat and allow to cool. Once cool, pour into a re-sealable container or a corked bottle and store in the refrigerator or behind your bar for regular use. This syrup will now last indefinitely.

SWEET AND SOUR MIX

To make sweet and sour mix, bring one cup of sugar syrup to simmer then add half a cup of fresh

lemon juice and half a cup of fresh lime juice. Simmer until well mixed, stirring frequently, then remove from heat and allow to cool. Once cool, pour into a re-sealable container or corked bottle and store in the refrigerator for up to two weeks. Sweet and sour mix is also referred to as sour mix or bar mix.

HOW TO CHILL A GLASS

Place bowls, jugs and glasses in a refrigerator to chill or place ice cubes into the glasses while drinks are being prepared. Discard these ice cubes before pouring unless otherwise instructed.

FRUIT, PEELS AND JUICES

Fruit slices and pieces will keep fresher and longer if covered with a damp, clean, linen cloth and refrigerated. Where citrus peel is required, cut the peel into required sizes and shave away the white membrane. Fruit and peels should be the last added ingredient to a cocktail or punch (garnish). When juices are required remember—fresh is best. When using canned fruit and/or juices, transfer the can's contents into appropriate re-sealable containers and refrigerate.

ICE

It is important to maintain a well-stocked, clean ice supply, as most cocktails and punches require ice during construction. To obtain crushed ice if you do not have access to an ice-crushing machine, place required ice onto a clean linen cloth and fold up. Place ice-filled cloth onto a hard surface and smash with a mallet—not a bottle.

Large blocks of ice are often required for punches. These ice blocks can be made easily by using two litre and/or four litre empty ice-cream containers.

GLASSWARE

Glasses come in a wide variety of shapes and sizes and range in value depending upon the quality of glass. When washing glasses, use hot water without detergent as detergent can distort the flavour of a drink or reduce the fizz in an effervescent drink. Only wash one glass at a time and dry with a clean lint-free cloth. Before using a glass, give it a quick polish with a glass cloth and check glass for chips and/or cracks. When handling glassware, hold glasses by their base or stem, as this will avoid finger marks around the rim of glass, thus maintaining a high polish.

The following is a list of glassware required for jugs and punches, although, for the home bar an extensive range of glassware is not always necessary. As an example, a wine glass could be used as a cocktail glass.

Beer	210ml (7fl oz)—375ml (13fl oz)
Champagne Saucer	140ml (4⅔fl oz)—180ml (6fl oz)
Cocktail	90ml (3fl oz)—140ml (4⅔fl oz)
Coffee	250ml (8⅓fl oz)
Goblet	140ml (4⅔fl oz)—285ml (9½fl oz)
Jug	Various Sizes
Old-Fashioned	180ml (6fl oz)—290ml (9⅔fl oz)
Punch Bowl	Various Sizes
Wine	150ml (5fl oz)—210ml (7fl oz)

BAR EQUIPMENT

Before purchasing any bar equipment, have a search through your kitchen as the majority of households contain a selection of items required for your bar. The following is a list of the most essential equipment.

Blender	Corkscrew	Knives	Spoons
Bottle Opener	Cutting Board	Mixing Glass	Stirrers
Bottle Stoppers	Fruit Juicer	Napkins	Straws
Can Opener	Glass Cloth	Soda Siphon	Swizzle Sticks
Coasters	Hawthorn Strainer	Spirit Measures	Toothpicks
Cocktail Shaker	Ice Bucket and Tongs	Sponge	

SETTING UP YOUR OWN BAR

Before you buy a bar, it's a good idea to visit pubs, clubs or cocktail bars or friends who may have home bars. This will give you lots of ideas on the different styles of bars and what sort of bar would best suit you and your home. This will also provide you with ideas on lighting, what different styles and types of bars have in common, in relation to their layout, size, etc, and what appeals to you personally. Also, take into consideration how much room you have for a bar and your budget.

There are many different sizes and styles of bars. The three main categories are:

MOBILE BAR

A mobile bar can be easily moved to any position you wish to serve from. For example, room to room or indoors to outdoors.

SEMI-PERMANENT BAR

This type of bar is the main feature of a room and is intended as a showpiece where glassware and bottles can be displayed. Erect this bar as close to washing-up facilities as is practical.

PERMANENT BAR

With only a few additions, you can turn a room into a bar. All you need is a built-in sink behind the bar with hot and cold water, a fridge/freezer, equipment and accessories. Glass shelving with mirrored backing provides the opportunity to place your glassware and bottles on display. Mood lighting can be used to great effect in such a room. Adding a couple of matching bar stools and a couple of lounges makes it the perfect room for retiring after that long day's work, not to mention holding cocktail parties in style.

COMMON INGREDIENTS
FOR JUGS AND PUNCHES

SPIRITS

Bacardi

Bourbon

Brandy

Canadian Whisky

Cognac

Dark Rum

Gin

Irish Whiskey

Light Rum

Port

Rye Whiskey

Scotch Whisky

Sherry

Tequila

Vodka

LIQUEURS

Amaretto

Bailey's Irish Cream

Banana Liqueur

Bénédictine

Cherry Brandy

Cointreau

Crème De Cacao

Crème De Cassis

Crème De Menthe

Curaçao

Drambuie

Galliano

Grand Marnier

Kirsch

Malibu

Midori

Southern Comfort

Strawberry Liqueur

Tia Maria

COMMON MIXERS

Apple Juice	Ginger Beer	Milk	Soda Water
Apricot Nectar	Grapefruit Juice	Mineral Water	Spring Water
Coconut Cream	Grape Juice	Orange Juice	Sweet and Sour Mix
Cola	Honey	Orange Soda	Tea
Cranberry Juice	Lemonade	Papaya Juice	Tomato Juice
Cream	Lemon Juice	Passionfruit Juice	Vanilla Ice Cream
Dry Ginger Ale	Lemon-Lime Soda	Peach Nectar	Worcestershire Sauce
Egg Nog	Lime Juice	Pineapple Juice	
Eggs	Mango Juice	Raspberry Syrup	

COMMON GARNISHES AND ADDITIVES

Almonds	Cucumber	Melon	Raspberries
Apples	Ginger	Nutmeg	Salt
Bananas	Honeydew Melon	Oranges	Sprigs of Mint
Blueberries	Kiwi Fruit	Paw Paw	Strawberries
Butter	Lemons	Peaches	Sugar
Cherries	Limes	Pepper	
Cinnamon	Mangoes	Pineapple	
Cloves	Maraschino Cherries	Raisins	

HOSTING A PARTY

Here are some helpful hints so that you and your guests enjoy your next party or occasion.

It's a great idea (and a time-saver) to pre-cut your fruit for garnishes and wrap them in plastic or place a clean, damp linen cloth over them and refrigerate until required. Juices should be squeezed and/or removed from tin cans/packet. Pour juices into re-sealable containers and refrigerate. Make up a bowl of sugar syrup and sweet and sour mix as described under Useful

Tips. This will save you from having to dissolve sugar when preparing large quantities of drinks. Keep a glass of water on your bar for rinsing instruments such as spoons and stirrers. If your washing machine is close to your bar or kitchen, fill it with clean, fresh ice. This will keep the ice chilled and will mean less mess to clean up during and after your party. As well as having a good supply of alcohol, make sure you have a fair selection of non-alcoholic drinks for those guests who prefer them.

If you find yourself hosting a large party, make yourself a checklist of what you require and what must be completed. Once your list is all checked off, you should then be able to sit down and relax before your guests arrive. Then you can enjoy delectable cocktails with family and friends without the stress of hosting the occasion.

CORDIALS AND LIQUEURS

Cordials and liqueurs are alcohol-based, with herbs, aromatic plants, essences, juices, beans, nuts, dairy products, sweeteners and colours infused in the spirit by the process of steeping and distillation.

Cordials and liqueurs date back centuries. In 1510, Bénédictine D.O.M. was created by a Benedictine monk, making it one of the world's oldest known liqueurs. The recipe for Bénédictine still remains a closely guarded secret as is the case for many cordials and liqueurs.

Traditionally, cordials and liqueurs were created for medicinal purposes as a cure for all types of ills. Creating cordials and liqueurs hundreds of years ago meant that people would gather herbs, fruits and plants from their gardens and then added them with sugar to liquors such as Gin or Brandy. Today, cordials and liqueurs are produced by distilling companies worldwide. It would not be possible to list all cordials and liqueurs that are available. A list of the main ones that are required for jugs and punches is provided in the introduction of this book.

Cordials and liqueurs are essential ingredients in a vast variety of cocktails, jugs and punches.

JUGS AND PUNCHES

Punches are believed to have originated in Jamaica in the mid-seventeenth century and were rum-based. The oldest-known punch contained only four ingredients: rum, orange juice, water and sugar.

Punches are great drinks for parties and place less demand on your time as you are not mixing individual drinks. They can be made, or at least prepared, before your guests arrive, giving you extra time to socialise and enjoy yourself. Punches can be made up simply in jugs or punch bowls, with fresh, seasonal fruit added and served with a ladle from a punch bowl or simply poured from a jug.

Ideally for cold punches, ingredients should be pre-chilled and large blocks of ice placed in the punch bowl will keep your punch cold. Empty ice-cream containers filled with water and frozen make ideal blocks of ice for punches. These large blocks will ensure that your punch will remain colder for a longer period of time for your guests to enjoy. Ice can be placed into jugs for the same effect. Effervescent ingredients should be added last into a punch apart from the fruit, unless otherwise stated.

When preparing a jug or punch allow 150ml (5fl oz) of drink per guest. This should provide you with an adequate amount, as some guests may choose not to drink alcohol or indulge in your punch.

EXTRA RECIPES

Some recipes call for extra items to be included with the drink.

SPICED WALNUTS

10ml (⅓fl oz) spring water
225g (½lb) walnuts
1 cup sugar
White of 1 egg
1 tablespoon cinnamon (ground)
¼ teaspoon cloves (ground)
Pinch of nutmeg

Pour egg white into a mixing bowl and beat until slightly frothy. Add water and stir well. Add walnuts and stir gently then strain thoroughly. Combine sugar, cinnamon, cloves and nutmeg into a separate bowl.

Preheat oven to 140°C (275°F). Dip walnuts into sugar mixture to coat thoroughly. Place coated walnuts onto a baking tray and bake for 20 minutes until golden brown.

Remove from tray and allow to cool to room temperature, then store in an air-tight container.

TOASTED ALMONDS

Almonds
Butter

Preheat oven to 140°C (275°F).

Place desired amount of almonds on a baking tray and coat with butter. Place tray into preheated oven and bake for 10 minutes turning once, almonds are baked once golden brown.

Remove from tray and allow to cool to room temperature then store in an air-tight container.

PINEAPPLE SHERBET

MAKES 1–1.25L/33.81-42.26FL OZ (DEPENDING ON SIZE OF PINEAPPLE)

375ml (13fl oz) fresh milk (chilled)
125ml (4fl oz) sugar syrup
36ml (1 fl oz) fresh lemon juice
1 fresh pineapple (diced)
Pinch of salt

Place diced pineapple into a blender without ice and blend well to purée then strain through a sieve, with force, into a container. Pour milk, sugar and juice into a mixing bowl. Add purée and a pinch of salt. Beat well to combine ingredients then pour into a container and cover. Place into refrigerator to chill for approximately 4 hours then freeze for approximately 1 hour prior to serving.

DAIRY EGG NOG

MAKES 2–2.25L/67.62-76.08FL OZ (DEPENDING ON SIZE OF EGGS)

1.5L (52fl oz) fresh milk (chilled)
2 tablespoons vanilla extract
3¼ cups caster sugar
12 fresh eggs
½ teaspoon cinnamon (ground)
½ teaspoon nutmeg (ground)
½ teaspoon salt

Pour eggs into a mixing bowl and beat well. Add extract, sugar, cinnamon, nutmeg and salt then beat well to mix. Add milk and stir well to combine ingredients. Pour into a jug and cover then refrigerate to chill.

Ideally this drink should be chilled for 24 hours prior to serving, as this will enhance the flavour.

FRUIT

ORCHARD PUNCH

MAKES 3.72L/125.95FL OZ | 11% ALC/VOL | 32.3 STANDARD DRINKS

1L (32fl oz) applejack

15ml (½fl oz) orange bitters

60ml (2fl oz) grenadine

500ml (17fl oz) fresh orange juice

150ml (5fl oz) grapefruit juice

1L (32fl oz) dry ginger ale

1L (32fl oz) lemon-lime soda

1 apple (sliced thinly)

1 fresh orange (sliced thinly)

Pour applejack, bitters, grenadine and juices into a chilled punch bowl. Stir well then add ginger ale and soda. Stir gently and add a large block of ice. Add slices of apple and orange then serve.

PUNCH ON THE NOSE

MAKES 1.96L/66.27FL OZ | 3.3% ALC/VOL | 7 STANDARD DRINKS

750ml (26fl oz) white wine (chilled)

375ml (13fl oz) pineapple juice

90ml (3fl oz) fresh lemon juice

750ml (26fl oz) soda water

Dash orange syrup/cordial

1 paw paw (diced)

Slices of orange

Slices of pineapple

Strawberries

Pour juices and syrup into a blender over cracked ice then add diced paw paw. Blend and pour into a chilled punch bowl. Add wine and stir thoroughly then refrigerate for three hours. Add ice, soda, slices of orange, pineapple and strawberries. Stir gently and serve.

FRUIT JUICE CUP

MAKES 2.69L/90.95FL OZ | 4.5% ALC/VOL | 9.6 STANDARD DRINKS

700ml (24fl oz) red lambrusco (sparkling)
100ml (3⅓fl oz) dark rum
500ml (17fl oz) fresh orange juice
200ml (7fl oz) pineapple juice
100ml (3⅓fl oz) sugar syrup
90ml (3fl oz) fresh lemon juice
1L (32fl oz) dry ginger ale
Slices of lemon
Slices of orange

Pour rum, juices and sugar syrup into a punch bowl over ice then stir well. Add ginger ale and lambrusco then stir gently. Add slices of lemon and orange then serve.

CAPE CODDER PUNCH

MAKES 5.27L/178.19FL OZ | 5.5% ALC/VOL | 22.9 STANDARD DRINKS

750ml (26fl oz) vodka
3L (104fl oz) cranberry-apple juice
500ml (17fl oz) fresh orange juice
180ml (6fl oz) sugar syrup
90ml (3fl oz) fresh lemon juice
750ml (26fl oz) mineral water

Pour vodka, juices and sugar into a chilled punch bowl. Stir well and refrigerate to chill. Add mineral water, stir gently and serve.

TROPICAL PUNCH

MAKES 3.45L/116.65 | 10.8% ALC/VOL | 29.4 STANDARD DRINKS

700ml (24fl oz) golden rum

500ml (17fl oz) apricot liqueur

750ml (26fl oz) grapefruit juice

750ml (26fl oz) pineapple juice

300ml (10fl oz) fresh orange juice

200ml (7fl oz) papaya juice

100ml (3⅓fl oz) mango juice

100ml (3⅓fl oz) passionfruit juice

50ml (1⅔fl oz) fresh lemon juice

Slices of orange

Slices of pineapple

Pour rum, liqueur and juices into a punch bowl over ice. Add slices of orange and pineapple.
Stir and serve.

FRUIT PUNCH

MAKES 4.86L/164.33 | 6.5% ALC/VOL | 26.5 STANDARD DRINKS

2L (64fl oz) white wine
250ml (8⅓fl oz) brandy
750ml (26fl oz) pineapple juice
500ml (17fl oz) fresh orange juice
240ml (8fl oz) fresh lemon juice
120ml (4fl oz) sugar syrup
1L (32fl oz) soda water
1½ cups peach slices
1 cup pineapple pieces
1 punnet cherries

Pour brandy, orange juice, lemon juice and sugar into a chilled punch bowl. Add slices of peach, pieces of pineapple and cherries. Stir and refrigerate for one hour. Add ice, wine, pineapple juice and soda. Stir gently and serve.

MINT PUNCH

MAKES 1.97L/66.61FL OZ | 3% ALC/VOL | 4.7 STANDARD DRINKS

120ml (4fl oz) Gin
60ml (2fl oz) Green Crème De Menthe
1L (32fl oz) pineapple juice
500ml (17fl oz) grapefruit juice
240ml (8fl oz) fresh lemon juice
50ml (1⅔fl oz) sugar syrup
Fresh mint leaves

Pour gin, Crème De Menthe, juices and sugar syrup into a punch bowl over ice. Stir well and float mint leaves on top, then serve.

PUNCH BOWLER

MAKES 1.75L/59.17 | 16% ALC/VOL | 22.1 STANDARD DRINKS

750ml (26fl oz) vodka
750ml (26fl oz) fresh orange juice
250ml (8⅓fl oz) grapefruit juice
Slices of orange

Pour vodka and juices into a punch bowl over ice then add slices of orange. Stir and serve.

POOR MAN'S PUNCH

MAKES 5.15L/174.14 |4.5% ALC/VOL | 18.2 STANDARD DRINKS

2L (64fl oz) red bordeaux wine
580ml (19fl oz) fresh lemon juice
285ml (9½fl oz) raspberry syrup
285ml (9½fl oz) sugar syrup
2L (64fl oz) soda water

Pour wine, juice, syrup and sugar syrup into a punch bowl over ice. Stir well and add soda. Stir gently and serve.

WEST INDIAN PUNCH

MAKES 6.08L/205.58FL OZ | 15% ALC/VOL | 71.6 STANDARD DRINKS

2L (64fl oz) light rum

750ml (26fl oz) banana liqueur

1L (32fl oz) fresh lemon juice

1L (32fl oz) fresh orange juice

1L (32fl oz) pineapple juice

150ml (5fl oz) sugar syrup

180ml (6fl oz) soda water

1 teaspoon cinnamon (ground)

1 teaspoon nutmeg (grated)

½ teaspoon cloves (ground)

Slices of banana

Pour sugar syrup and soda into a jug without ice. Add cinnamon, nutmeg and cloves. Stir gently and pour into a punch bowl over a large block of ice. Add remaining ingredients, stir and serve.

POLYNESIAN
PUNCH BOWL

MAKES 4.44L/150.13FL OZ | 10% ALC/VOL | 35 STANDARD DRINKS

750ml (26fl oz) light rum

540ml (18fl oz) sloe gin

150ml (5fl oz) peppermint schnapps

1.25L (42fl oz) pineapple juice

750ml (26fl oz) fresh orange juice

250ml (8⅓fl oz) fresh lemon juice

180ml (6fl oz) coconut cream (chilled)

570ml (19fl oz) soda water

12 thin slices of orange

12 thin slices of pineapple

Pour rum, gin, schnapps, juices and cream into a chilled punch bowl then stir well to blend cream. Add a large block of ice, slices of orange and pineapple then refrigerate for one hour. Add soda, stir gently and serve.

BARBADOS BOWL

MAKES 3.70L/125.11FL OZ | 13% ALC/VOL | 36.6 STANDARD DRINKS

750ml (26fl oz) light rum
240ml (8fl oz) 151-proof rum
1.36L (46fl oz) pineapple juice
360ml (12fl oz) mango nectar
250ml (8⅓fl oz) fresh lime juice
1 cup sugar
6 bananas (diced)
2 bananas (sliced)
2 fresh limes (sliced)

Pour lime juice into a blender without ice then add sugar and diced banana. Blend until smooth and pour into a punch bowl over a large block of ice. Add rums, pineapple juice and nectar then stir well. Add slices of banana and lime then serve.

ORANGE PUNCH

MAKES 3L/101.44FL OZ | 9.3% ALC/VOL | 22 STANDARD DRINKS

750ml (26fl oz) vodka
750ml (26fl oz) fresh orange juice
750ml (26fl oz) dry ginger ale
750ml (26fl oz) soda water

Pour vodka and juice into a punch bowl over ice then stir. Add ginger ale and soda. Stir gently and serve.

RUM AND FRUIT JUICE BOWL

MAKES 1.40L/47.33FL OZ | 9.4% ALC/VOL | 10.5 STANDARD DRINKS

360ml (12fl oz) dark rum
60ml (2fl oz) grenadine
300ml (10fl oz) fresh orange juice
300ml (10fl oz) pineapple juice
180ml (6fl oz) fresh lemon juice
180ml (6fl oz) coconut cream
30ml (1fl oz) sugar syrup
Maraschino cherries
Pieces of pineapple

Pour rum, grenadine, juices, cream and sugar syrup into a punch bowl over ice. Add cherries and pieces of pineapple. Stir well and serve.

MELON BALL CUP

MAKES 1.36L/ 45.98FL OZ | 12.5% ALC/VOL | 13.5 STANDARD DRINKS

375ml (13fl oz) Midori
240ml (8fl oz) vodka
750ml (26fl oz) fresh orange juice or grapefruit juice
Slices of melon
Slices of orange
Strawberries

Pour Midori, vodka and juice into a jug over ice then add remaining ingredients. Stir and serve.

RED RUBY FROST PUNCH

MAKES 1.42L/48FL OZ | 6.2% ALC/VOL | 7.9 STANDARD DRINKS

500ml (17fl oz) raspberry schnapps
500ml (17fl oz) cranberry juice
360ml (12fl oz) fresh lemon juice
60ml (2fl oz) dry ginger ale
1 cup caster sugar

Pour juices into a blender without ice and add sugar. Blend well and pour into a jug over ice. Add schnapps and ginger ale. Stir well and serve.

EXTRA-KICK PUNCH

MAKES 3.31L/111.92FL OZ | 8% ALC/VOL | 22.4 STANDARD DRINKS

500ml (17fl oz) dark rum
250ml (8⅓fl oz) brandy
60ml (2fl oz) peach brandy
2L (64fl oz) spring water
250ml (8⅓fl oz) fresh lemon juice
250ml (8⅓fl oz) pineapple juice
1 cup brown sugar

Pour water into a mixing bowl without ice. Add sugar then stir well to dissolve sugar. Add remaining ingredients, stir and refrigerate to chill. Pour into a punch bowl over a large block of ice and serve.

PHI BETA BLUEBERRY

MAKES 4.07L/137.62FL OZ | 13.5% ALC/VOL | 43.4 STANDARD DRINKS

750ml (26fl oz) 100-proof vodka
480ml (16fl oz) Metaxa Brandy
480ml (16fl oz) blueberry syrup
360ml (12fl oz) fresh lemon juice
2l (64fl oz) soda water
2 fresh lemons (sliced thinly)
1 punnet blueberries

Pour vodka, Brandy, syrup and juice into a punch bowl over a large block of ice. Stir and refrigerate for one hour. Add soda and stir gently. Float slices of lemon and blueberries on top then serve.

ORANGE ALMOND BOWL

MAKES 3.9L/131.87FL OZ | 10% ALC/VOL | 30.7 STANDARD DRINKS

540ml (18fl oz) blended whiskey
360ml (12fl oz) danish aquavit
240ml (8fl oz) sweet vermouth
5ml (1/6fl oz) orange bitters
1.5L (52fl oz) quinine water
1.25L (42fl oz) fresh orange juice
170g (6oz) toasted almonds (slivered)
Peel of 2 fresh oranges (cut into strips)

Pour whiskey, aquavit, vermouth, bitters and juice into a punch bowl over a large block of ice. Stir and refrigerate for one hour. Add quinine water and stir. Float almonds and orange peel on top then serve.

See page 22 for a recipe for toasted almonds.

RUM PUNCH

MAKES 1.42L/48FL OZ | 7.5% ALC/VOL | 9.1 STANDARD DRINKS

300ml (10fl oz) Bacardi
180ml (6fl oz) fresh lemon juice
180ml (6fl oz) fresh orange juice
120ml (4fl oz) pineapple juice
750ml (26fl oz) dry ginger ale
Slices of lemon
Slices of orange

Pour Bacardi and juices into a punch bowl over ice then stir. Add ginger ale and stir gently. Add slices of lemon and orange then serve.

CAPE COD CRANBERRY PUNCH

MAKES 3.9L/131.87FL OZ | 14.3% ALC/VOL | 43.9 STANDARD DRINKS

1L (32fl oz) 100-proof vodka
180ml (6fl oz) cherry liqueur
2L (64fl oz) cranberry juice
700ml (24fl oz) fresh orange juice
15ml (½fl oz) orange flower water
2 fresh limes (sliced thinly)
1 teaspoon cinnamon
½ teaspoon allspice
¼ teaspoon nutmeg

Place cinnamon, allspice and nutmeg into a mixing glass without ice. Add a small quantity of vodka and stir to a paste. Pour remaining vodka, liqueur, juices and flower water into a punch bowl over a large block of ice then stir well. Add prepared paste and stir well. Float slices of lime on top and serve.

CITRUS-BEER PUNCH

MAKES 1.5L/50.72FL OZ | 1.1% ALC/VOL | 1.5 STANDARD DRINKS

750ml (26fl oz) light beer
500ml (17fl oz) sugar syrup
250ml (8⅓fl oz) grapefruit juice
8 fresh lemons (juiced and peeled)
Slices of lemon

Pour sugar syrup into a saucepan and bring to the boil then add lemon peel. Remove from heat, cover and allow to stand for five minutes. Strain into a jug and add juices then stir. Cover and refrigerate to chill. Add beer and stir gently. Pour into glass beer mugs over cracked ice and garnish with a slice of lemon for each serving.

RUM PUNCH GRANDE

MAKES 16.5L/557.93FL OZ | 16% ALC/VOL | 241 STANDARD DRINKS

7.5L (256fl oz) white wine

4.5L (150fl oz) light rum

750ml (26fl oz) banana liqueur

750ml (26fl oz) Jamaica rum

2L (64fl oz) fresh orange juice

1L (32fl oz) fresh lemon juice

10 bananas (sliced)

2 pineapples (diced)

900g (2lb) brown sugar

Pour wine and juices into a crockpot. Add slices of banana, diced pineapple and sugar. Stir and cover then allow to stand overnight. Add rums and liqueur then stir. Strain into a punch bowl over a large block of ice and serve.

CLARET PUNCH

MAKES 4.86L/164.33FL OZ | 6.5% ALC/VOL | 24.9 STANDARD DRINKS

2L (64fl oz) claret
250ml (8⅓fl oz) brandy
750ml (26fl oz) pineapple juice
500ml (17fl oz) fresh orange juice
240ml (8fl oz) fresh lemon juice
120ml (4fl oz) sugar syrup
1L (32fl oz) soda water
2 fresh lemons (sliced)
1 pineapple (sliced)

Pour brandy, orange juice, lemon juice and sugar syrup into a chilled punch bowl. Add slices of lemon and pineapple. Stir well and refrigerate for one hour. Add ice, claret, pineapple juice and soda. Stir gently and serve.

PINEAPPLE AND ORANGE PUNCH

MAKES 1.86L/62.89FL OZ | 7.5% ALC/VOL | 11 STANDARD DRINKS

375ml (13fl oz) dry gin
375ml (13fl oz) fresh orange juice
180ml (6fl oz) fresh lemon juice
180ml (6fl oz) pineapple juice
750ml (26fl oz) lemonade or soda water
Slices of orange
Slices of pineapple
Strawberries

Pour gin and juices into a punch bowl over ice. Add slices of orange, pineapple and strawberries. Stir and add lemonade or soda as desired. Stir gently and serve.

INTERPLANETARY PUNCH

MAKES 3.47L/117.33FL OZ | 13.5% ALC/VOL | 28.1 STANDARD DRINKS

750ml (26fl oz) light rum

360ml (12fl oz) peppermint schnapps

1L (32fl oz) fresh orange juice

1L (32fl oz) mango nectar

360ml (12fl oz) thick cream (chilled)

1 fresh mango (sliced)

6 orange quarters

Leaves from 8 sprigs of fresh mint

Pour schnapps, juice, nectar and cream into a punch bowl over a large block of ice. Stir well then float slices of mango, orange and mint leaves on top. Refrigerate for one hour then stir and serve.

ALL-AMERICAN PUNCH

MAKES 3.18L/107.52FL OZ | 5.3% ALC/VOL | 13.3 STANDARD DRINKS

450ml (15fl oz) Southern Comfort

450ml (15fl oz) fresh orange juice

90ml (3fl oz) fresh lime juice

30ml (1fl oz) maraschino cherry juice

1.8L (60fl oz) cola

360ml (12fl oz) soda water

Maraschino cherries

Slices of lime

Slices of orange

Pour Southern Comfort and juices into a chilled punch bowl. Stir well and add a large block of ice.
Add cola and soda then stir gently. Add cherries, slices of lime and orange then serve.

MAUI WOWIE PUNCH

MAKES 4.45L/150.47FL OZ | 10.5% ALC/VOL | 37.3 STANDARD DRINKS

1.7L (58fl oz) Malibu
500ml (17fl oz) Midori
1.125L (38fl oz) fresh lemon juice
1.125L (38fl oz) pineapple juice
Slices of orange
Slices of pineapple

Pour Malibu, Midori and juices into a punch bowl over ice then stir well. Add slices of orange and pineapple then serve.

DUTCH APPLE PUNCH

MAKES 3.9L/131.87FL OZ | 1.7% ALC/VOL | 5.2 STANDARD DRINKS

1.4L (50fl oz) cider (chilled)
2L (64fl oz) apple juice
500ml (17fl oz) fresh orange juice
2 cinnamon sticks

Pour juices into a chilled punch bowl and stir. Add cinnamon sticks and refrigerate for two hours. Remove cinnamon sticks and add cider. Place punch bowl on a bed of ice, stir gently and serve.

DANCING DUTCHMAN

MAKES 2.7L/91.29FL OZ |3.9% ALC/VOL | 8.3 STANDARD DRINKS

250ml (8⅓fl oz) white wine
125ml (4fl oz) vodka
75ml (2½fl oz) scotch whisky
1.25L (42fl oz) strawberry juice
750ml (26fl oz) peach nectar
250ml (8⅓fl oz) fresh lime juice
Cherries

Pour juices and nectar into a blender over crushed ice. blend until slushy then add wine, vodka and whisky. blend and pour into a chilled punch bowl. add cherries and serve.

FOREPLAY ON THE NEUTRAL GROUND

MAKES 1.08L/36.51FL OZ | 10.5% ALC/VOL | 8.9 STANDARD DRINKS

240ml (8fl oz) vodka
120ml (4fl oz) Midori
360ml (12fl oz) cranberry juice
360ml (12fl oz) pineapple juice

Pour ingredients into a jug over ice and stir well then serve in glasses filled with ice.

MALIBU PARTY PUNCH

MAKES 8.13L/274.90FL OZ | 4.5% ALC/VOL | 28.8 STANDARD DRINKS

1.75L (58fl oz) Malibu
2.25L (72fl oz) cranberry-raspberry juice
1.125L (38fl oz) fresh lime juice
3L (104fl oz) soda water
Slices of lime
Slices of orange

Pour Malibu and juices into a punch bowl over a large block of ice. Add soda and stir gently. Add slices of lime and orange then serve.

PEACH ON
THE BEACH PUNCH

MAKES 4.25L/143.70FL OZ | 13.4% ALC/VOL | 44.9 STANDARD DRINKS

1.75L (58fl oz) Malibu
1L (32fl oz) peach schnapps
1.5L (52fl oz) fresh orange juice
Slices of orange
Slices of peach

Pour Malibu, schnapps and juice into a punch bowl over a large block of ice then stir. Add slices of orange and peach then serve.

CANNONBALL

MAKES 3.98L/134.57FL OZ | 9.5% ALC/VOL | 29.8 STANDARD DRINKS

500ml (17fl oz) light rum
500ml (17fl oz) gin
1L (32fl oz) fresh orange juice
1L (32fl oz) pineapple juice
620ml (20fl oz) lemon-lime soda
360ml (12fl oz) strawberry soda

Pour rum, gin and juices into a punch bowl resting on a bed of ice. Stir well and add sodas. Stir gently and serve.

HALL OF FAME PUNCH

MAKES 0.96L/32.46FL OZ | 7% ALC/VOL | 5.3 STANDARD DRINKS

180ml (6fl oz) vodka
60ml (2fl oz) grenadine
180ml (6fl oz) fresh orange juice
180ml (6fl oz) pineapple juice
180ml (6fl oz) sweet and sour mix
180ml (6fl oz) lemon-lime soda
Cherries
Slices of orange

Pour Vodka, Grenadine, juices and sour mix into a jug over large amount of ice then stir well. Add soda and stir gently. Add cherries and slices of orange then serve.

AMBROSIA PUNCH

MAKES 2.83L/95.69FL OZ | 4.1% ALC/VOL | 11.3 STANDARD DRINKS

375ml (13fl oz) light rum
500ml (17fl oz) apricot nectar
500ml (17fl oz) fresh orange juice
450ml (15fl oz) coconut cream
1L (32fl oz) soda water
1 pineapple (diced)

Pour cream into a blender without ice and add diced pineapple. Blend well and pour into a punch bowl over ice. Add Rum, nectar and juice. Stir and add soda. Stir gently and serve.

ALABAMA SLAMMER SP STYLE

MAKES 2L/67.62FL OZ | 12.8% ALC/VOL | 37 STANDARD DRINKS

500ml (17fl oz) Southern Comfort
250ml (8⅓fl oz) Amaretto
1L (32fl oz) cranberry juice
250ml (8⅓fl oz) fresh orange juice

Pour ingredients into a jug over ice, stir well and serve.

SWINGIN' IN THE TREES

MAKES 5.75L/194.43FL OZ | 8.9% ALC/VOL | 40.4 STANDARD DRINKS

750ml (26fl oz) light rum
500ml (17fl oz) curaçao
500ml (17fl oz) Malibu
750ml (26fl oz) grape juice
750ml (26fl oz) fresh orange juice
750ml (26fl oz) pineapple juice
1L (32fl oz) lime soda
750ml (26fl oz) lemonade

Pour rum, curaçao, Malibu and juices into a chilled punch bowl. Stir well and refrigerate to chill. Add ice, soda and lemonade. Stir gently and serve.

SIMPSON SOLUTION

MAKES 9L/304.32FL OZ | 4.8% ALC/VOL | 44 STANDARD DRINKS

750ml (26fl oz) peach schnapps
750ml (26fl oz) vodka
7.5L (266fl oz) fresh orange juice

Pour ingredients into a large punch bowl over ice, stir and serve.

SUN BURN PUNCH

MAKES 4.5L/152.16FL OZ | 12.3% ALC/VOL | 43.7 STANDARD DRINKS

1.5L (52fl oz) vodka
1.5L (52fl oz) cranberry juice
1.5L (52fl oz) grapefruit juice
Cherries
Slices of lime

Pour vodka and juices into a punch bowl over a large block of ice then stir well.
Add cherries and slices of lime then serve.

TROPICAL HOOTER PUNCH

MAKES 3.61L/122.06FL OZ | 12.3% ALC/VOL | 35 STANDARD DRINKS

1.75L (58fl oz) Malibu
360ml (12fl oz) Midori
750ml (26fl oz) cranberry juice
750ml (26fl oz) pineapple juice
Cherries
Slices of orange

Pour Malibu, Midori and juices into a punch bowl over ice then stir well. Add cherries and slices of orange then serve.

BLUE HAWAIIAN PUNCH

MAKES 4.25L/143.70FL OZ | 14.6% ALC/VOL | 49 STANDARD DRINKS

1.75L (58fl oz) Malibu
1L (32fl oz) blue curaçao
1.5L (52fl oz) pineapple juice
Pineapple pieces

Pour Malibu, curaçao and juice into a punch bowl over a large block of ice then add pieces of pineapple. Stir and serve.

ERNIE'S KILLER PUNCH

MAKES 2.22L/75.06FL OZ | 12.4% ALC/VOL | 21.7 STANDARD DRINKS

180ml (6fl oz) 151-proof rum

180ml (6fl oz) gin

180ml (6fl oz) Malibu

90ml (3fl oz) raspberry liqueur

90ml (3fl oz) tropical schnapps

750ml (26fl oz) cranberry-raspberry juice

750ml (26fl oz) pineapple juice

Pour ingredients into a large container without ice and shake well. Pour into a punch bowl over a large block of ice and serve.

TROPICAL PUNCH NO. 2

MAKES 8L/270.51FL OZ | 14.5% ALC/VOL | 95.8 STANDARD DRINKS

4.5L (150fl oz) white wine

1L (32fl oz) light rum

500ml (17fl oz) banana liqueur

500ml (17fl oz) dark rum

1L (32fl oz) fresh orange juice

500ml (17fl oz) fresh lemon juice

450g (1lb) brown sugar

5 bananas (sliced)

1 pineapple (diced)

Fresh fruit (diced)

Pour wine and juices into a chilled punch bowl add sugar, slices of banana and diced pineapple. cover and allow to stand for 12 hours. strain into a chilled punch bowl then add rums and liqueur. add a large block of ice and refrigerate for one hour. add diced fruit, stir gently and serve.

U-238 PUNCH

MAKES 3.75L/126.80FL OZ | 15% ALC/VOL | 44.4 STANDARD DRINKS

750ml (26fl oz) light rum
750ml (26fl oz) vodka
750ml (26fl oz) fresh orange juice
750ml (26fl oz) pineapple juice
750ml (26fl oz) strawberry juice
2 cups pineapple pieces
2 cups strawberries
2 cups wedges of orange

Pour rum, vodka and juices into a punch bowl resting on a bed of ice then stir well. Add pieces of pineapple, strawberries and wedges of orange then serve.

BOZO SWEET

MAKES 2.61L/88.25FL OZ | 25.7% ALC/VOL | 68.1 STANDARD DRINKS

750ml (26fl oz) everclear
750ml (26fl oz) peach schnapps
750ml (26fl oz) orange soda
360ml (12fl oz) grape kool-aid/cordial
1kg (2lb 4oz) sugar
Slices of orange
Slices of peach

Pour Everclear and schnapps into a punch bowl resting on a bed of ice then add sugar. Stir well and add kool-aid. Add soda and stir gently. Add slices of orange and peach then serve.

AMERICAN ICE TEA

MAKES 1.5L/50.72FL OZ | 5% ALC/VOL | 5.9 STANDARD DRINKS

300ml (10fl oz) triple sec
750ml (26fl oz) strong black tea (chilled)
450ml (15fl oz) fresh orange juice

Pour triple sec and juice into a jug over ice then stir. Add tea by layering on top and serve.

RUM-TA-TUM

MAKES 2L/67.62FL OZ | 7.1% ALC/VOL | 11.3 STANDARD DRINKS

375ml (13fl oz) light rum
15ml (½fl oz) grenadine
500ml (17fl oz) pineapple juice
120ml (4fl oz) fresh lemon juice
1L (32fl oz) soda water
Slices of orange

Pour rum, grenadine and juices into a jug over ice. Stir and add soda. Stir gently and garnish with a slice of orange for each serving.

BERRY DEADLY PUNCH

MAKES 7.75L/262.05FL OZ | 12.3% ALC/VOL | 75.2 STANDARD DRINKS

1L (32fl oz) Everclear

750ml (26fl oz) strawberry wine

2L (64fl oz) fresh orange juice

4L (132fl oz) lemonade

Pour Everclear, Wine and juice into a punch bowl resting on a bed of ice then stir. Add lemonade, stir gently and serve.

CHAMPAGNE

BOMBAY PUNCH

MAKES 8L/270.51FL OZ | 16% ALC/VOL | 47.7 STANDARD DRINKS

1.5L (52fl oz) champagne

750ml (26fl oz) brandy

750ml (26fl oz) sherry

15ml (½fl oz) cointreau

15ml (½fl oz) maraschino liqueur

750ml (26fl oz) soda water

Slices of kiwi fruit

Slices of lemon

Slices of orange

Pour brandy, sherry, cointreau and liqueur into a punch bowl over ice. add slices of kiwi fruit, lemon and orange. stir then add soda and champagne. stir gently and serve.

CHAMPAGNE PUNCH

MAKES 1.10L/37.19FL OZ | 11.5% ALC/VOL | 10 STANDARD DRINKS

750ml (26fl oz) champagne

60ml (2fl oz) brandy

45ml (1½fl oz) cointreau

250ml (8⅓fl oz) fresh orange juice

Maraschino cherries

Pieces of pineapple

Slices of orange

Pour brandy, cointreau and juice into a punch bowl over ice. add cherries, pieces of pineapple and slices of orange. stir well and add champagne. stir gently and serve.

BELLINI PUNCH

MAKES 1.53L/51.73FL OZ | 7.5% ALC/VOL | 14.4 STANDARD DRINKS

1.5L (52fl oz) champagne
30ml (1fl oz) fresh lemon juice
10 fresh peaches (diced)
Slices of peach

Pour juice into a blender over cracked ice and add diced peaches. Blend and pour into a punch bowl over ice. Add Champagne and stir gently. Add slices of peach and serve.

FLAMINGO PUNCH

MAKES 1.5L/50.72FL OZ | 12% ALC/VOL | 14.2 STANDARD DRINKS

750ml (26fl oz) champagne
750ml (26fl oz) crackling rosé wine
1 punnet raspberries

Place raspberries into a punch bowl over a large block of ice then add champagne and wine simultaneously. stir gently and serve.

PARTY PUNCH

MAKES 2.97L/100.42FL OZ | 17% ALC/VOL | 39.8 STANDARD DRINKS

1.5L (52fl oz) champagne
750ml (26fl oz) Southern Comfort
120ml (4fl oz) Jamaica rum
240ml (8fl oz) grapefruit juice
240ml (8fl oz) pineapple juice
120ml (4fl oz) fresh lemon juice
Slices of orange

Pour Southern Comfort, rum and juices into a punch bowl over ice then add slices of orange. stir well and add champagne. stir gently and serve.

NO. 1 BOOBY TRAP

MAKES 2.24L/75.74FL OZ | 21.4% ALC/VOL | 37.7 STANDARD DRINKS

750ml (26fl oz) champagne
375ml (13fl oz) Drambuie
375ml (13fl oz) Southern Comfort
180ml (6fl oz) Bacardi
180ml (6fl oz) Rosso Antico
375ml (13fl oz) fresh orange juice
Slices of lemon
Slices of orange
Strawberries

Pour Drambuie, Southern Comfort, Bacardi, Rosso Antico and juice into a punch bowl over ice. Add slices of lemon, orange and strawberries. Stir well and add champagne. Stir gently and serve.

CHAMPAGNE CUP

MAKES 0.85L/28.74FL OZ | 13% ALC/VOL | 8.8 STANDARD DRINKS

750ml (26fl oz) champagne
60ml (2fl oz) brandy
30ml (1fl oz) fresh lemon juice
15ml (½fl oz) sugar syrup
Pieces of pineapple
Slices of lemon
Slices of orange

Pour juice and sugar syrup into a mixing glass without ice. stir well and pour into a jug over ice then add brandy. add pieces of pineapple, slices of lemon and orange. stir and add champagne. stir gently and serve.

PARISIANA PUNCH

MAKES 1.2L/40.57FL OZ | 13% ALC/VOL | 14.9 STANDARD DRINKS

750ml (26fl oz) champagne

300ml (10fl oz) Madeira

150ml (5fl oz) cognac

½ cup sugar

2 fresh lemons (thinly sliced in halves)

Pour Madeira and cognac into a chilled jug then add sugar. Stir well to dissolve sugar and add slices of lemon then refrigerate for three hours. Add champagne, stir gently and serve.

CHAMPAGNE SHERBET PUNCH

MAKES 2.56L/86.56FL OZ | 3.5% ALC/VOL | 7.1 STANDARD DRINKS

750ml (26fl oz) champagne

750ml (26fl oz) pineapple juice (chilled)

60ml (2fl oz) fresh lemon juice

1L (32fl oz) pineapple sherbet (see recipe page 23)

Pour juices into a chilled punch bowl then add sherbet. Stir well and add champagne. Stir gently and serve.

PIMM'S PUNCH

MAKES 2.1L/71FL OZ | 19% ALC/VOL | 33.5 STANDARD DRINKS

750ml (26fl oz) champagne

375ml (13fl oz) Pimm's No.1

375ml (13fl oz) bourbon

180ml (6fl oz) light rum

180ml (6fl oz) sweet vermouth

300ml (10fl oz) fresh orange juice

75ml (2½fl oz) frozen orange concentrate

Slices of kiwi fruit

Slices of orange

Slices of pineapple

Strawberries

Pour Pimm's, bourbon, rum and vermouth into a punch bowl over ice. Add concentrate, slices of kiwi fruit, orange, pineapple and strawberries. Stir well, then add juice and Champagne.
Stir gently and serve.

SUNSET PUNCH

MAKES 3.1L/104.82FL OZ | 11% ALC/VOL | 29.4 STANDARD DRINKS

1.5L (52fl oz) champagne

240ml (8fl oz) Cointreau

180ml (6fl oz) maraschino liqueur

90ml (3fl oz) brandy

90ml (3fl oz) cherry brandy

500ml (17fl oz) fresh lemon juice

500ml (17fl oz) strong black tea (chilled)

1 cup caster sugar

24 maraschino cherries

2 fresh oranges (sliced)

Pour juice into a chilled punch bowl and add sugar then stir well to dissolve. Add Cointreau, liquour, brandies and tea then stir. Add a large block of ice and champagne then stir gently. Add cherries and slices of orange then serve.

CHARLESTON PUNCH

MAKES 7.25L/245.15FL OZ | 12.5% ALC/VOL | 74.5 STANDARD DRINKS

3L (104fl oz) champagne

750ml (26fl oz) brandy

500ml (17fl oz) dark rum

300ml (10fl oz) peach brandy

1.5L (52fl oz) soda water

1L (32fl oz) green tea (chilled)

3 cups sugar

10 fresh limes (sliced thinly)

1 pineapple (sliced thinly)

Pour brandy into a punch bowl then add slices of lime and pineapple. cover and allow to marinate overnight. add rum, peach brandy, tea and sugar. stir well to dissolve sugar and refrigerate for three hours. add soda and champagne. stir gently and serve.

TARTAN CHAMPAGNE PUNCH

MAKES 3.1L/104.82FL OZ | 12.5% ALC/VOL | 31.9 STANDARD DRINKS

2.25L (72fl oz) champagne

120ml (4fl oz) Drambuie

120ml (4fl oz) brandy

120ml (4fl oz) maraschino liqueur

500ml (17fl oz) soda water

½ cup sugar

1 fresh orange (peeled and sliced)

Pour Drambuie into a chilled punch bowl and add sugar. Stir well to dissolve sugar then add brandy, liqueur and soda. Stir and add champagne. Stir gently and add slices of orange then serve.

REGENT PUNCH

1.5L (52fl oz) champagne
570ml (19fl oz) Jamaica rum
113ml (3¾fl oz) brandy
113ml (3¾fl oz) swedish punsch
55ml (15/6fl oz) curaçao
5ml (1/6fl oz) Angostura Bitters
250ml (8⅓fl oz) strong black tea (chilled)
180ml (6fl oz) fresh lemon juice
Slices of lemon
Slices of orange
Strawberries

Pour rum, brandy, punsch, curaçao, Bitters, tea and juice into a punch bowl resting on a bed of ice. Add slices of lemon, orange and strawberries. Stir well and add Champagne. Stir gently and serve.

BOSTON PUNCH

MAKES 1.85L/62.55FL OZ | 11.5% ALC/VOL | 16.8 STANDARD DRINKS

750ml (26fl oz) champagne
280ml (9⅓fl oz) cider
140ml (4fl oz) brandy
90ml (3⅔fl oz) dark rum
60ml (2fl oz) Cointreau
120ml (4fl oz) fresh lemon juice
1 tablespoon sugar syrup
400ml (13⅓fl oz) soda water
1 apple (cut into wedges)

Pour cider, brandy, rum, Cointreau, juice and sugar syrup into a punch bowl over ice then stir. Add soda and champagne then stir gently. Add wedges of apple and serve.

BUDDHA PUNCH

MAKES 2.29L/77.43FL OZ | 7.5% ALC/VOL | 13.6 STANDARD DRINKS

750ml (26fl oz) champagne

250ml (8⅓fl oz) Rhine riesling

90ml (3fl oz) curaçao

90ml (3fl oz) rum

Dash Angostura Bitters

180ml (6fl oz) fresh lemon juice

180ml (6fl oz) fresh orange juice

750ml (26fl oz) soda water

Fresh mint leaves

Twists of lemon peel

Pour riesling, curaçao, rum, Bitters and juices into a punch bowl over a large block of ice. Stir and add soda. Add mint leaves, lemon peel and champagne. Stir gently and serve.

CREOLE CHAMPAGNE PUNCH

MAKES 3.93L/132.88FL OZ | 8% ALC/VOL | 26.4 STANDARD DRINKS

1.5L (52fl oz) champagne
750ml (26fl oz) dry white wine
120ml (4fl oz) Cointreau
60ml (2fl oz) brandy
500ml (17fl oz) fresh lemon juice
1L (32fl oz) soda water
1 cup caster sugar
½ pineapple (diced)
½ pineapple (sliced thinly)
2 punnets strawberries

Pour juice into a chilled punch bowl and add sugar then stir well to dissolve sugar. add wine, Cointreau, brandy, soda and diced pineapple. Stir and add champagne then stir gently. Add a large block of ice, slices of pineapple and strawberries then serve.

ROCKY MOUNTAIN PUNCH

MAKES 5.57L/188.34FL OZ | 14% ALC/VOL | 61.4 STANDARD DRINKS

4L (132fl oz) champagne
750ml (26fl oz) Jamaica rum
120ml (4fl oz) maraschino liqueur
580ml (19fl oz) fresh lemon juice
120ml (4fl oz) sugar syrup

Pour rum, liqueur, juice and sugar syrup into a blender over cracked ice. Blend and pour into a chilled punch bowl. Add champagne, stir gently and serve.

CHAMPAGNE SPRAY PUNCH

MAKES 3.06L/103.47FL OZ | 4.5% ALC/VOL | 11.1 STANDARD DRINKS

750ml (26fl oz) champagne
250ml (8⅓fl oz) Crème De Cassis
1L (32fl oz) cranberry juice
60ml (2fl oz) fresh lime juice
1L (32fl oz) soda water
4 tablespoons honey
Slices of lime

Pour lime juice and honey into a mixing glass without ice then stir well to dissolve honey. Pour Cassis, cranberry juice and soda into a punch bowl over ice. Stir and add honey mixture then stir again. Add champagne and slices of lime. Stir gently and serve.

VODKA BOMBAY PUNCH

MAKES 8.43L/285.05FL OZ | 13.5% ALC/VOL | 89.7 STANDARD DRINKS

4L (132fl oz) champagne
1L (32fl oz) vodka
1L (32fl oz) sherry
285ml (9½fl oz) curaçao
140ml (4⅔fl oz) maraschino liqueur
2L (64fl oz) soda water
Cherries
Slices of orange

Pour vodka, sherry, curaçao and liqueur into a punch bowl resting on a bed of ice. Add cherries and slices of orange. Stir then add soda and champagne. Stir gently and serve.

CHRISTMAS PUNCH

MAKES 4.86L/164.33FL OZ | 18.2% ALC/VOL | 98.5 STANDARD DRINKS

2L (64fl oz) champagne

750ml (26fl oz) brandy

750ml (26fl oz) rum

750ml (26fl oz) rye whiskey

375ml (13fl oz) Bénédictine

10ml (⅓fl oz) Angostura Bitters

1L (32fl oz) fresh orange juice

1L (32fl oz) strong black tea (chilled)

225ml (7½fl oz) sugar syrup

1 pineapple (diced)

Pour brandy, rum, whiskey, Bénédictine, Bitters, juice, tea and sugar syrup into a mixing bowl without ice then add diced pineapple. Stir well and pour into a punch bowl over a large block of ice then add champagne. Stir gently and serve.

KISSING THE BRIDE PUNCH

MAKES 1.68L/56.80FL OZ | 14.8% ALC/VOL | 19.8 STANDARD DRINKS

1.5L (52fl oz) champagne
180ml (6fl oz) cognac
1 tablespoon icing sugar
1 punnet strawberries

Place strawberries into a chilled punch bowl and sprinkle sugar over strawberries. Add cognac and refrigerate for eight hours. Add champagne, stir gently and serve.

CHAMPAGNE CONTINENTAL PUNCH

MAKES 5.96L/201.53FL OZ | 11.9% ALC/VOL | 78.2 STANDARD DRINKS

4L (132fl oz) champagne
570ml (19fl oz) cognac
570ml (19fl oz) Jamaica rum
113ml (3¾fl oz) curaçao
113ml (3¾fl oz) maraschino liqueur
600ml (20fl oz) fresh lemon juice
450g (1lb) caster sugar
3 pineapples (crushed)

Place crushed pineapple into a punch bowl and cover with sugar then allow to stand for one hour. Add Cognac, Rum, Curaçao, Liqueur and juice then stir well. Cover and allow to stand for 18 hours. Add a large block of ice and Champagne. Stir gently and serve.

CHAMPAGNE PINEAPPLE PUNCH

MAKES 1.64L/55.45FL OZ | 8.1% ALC/VOL | 11.9 STANDARD DRINKS

750ml (26fl oz) champagne
500ml (17fl oz) sauterne
300ml (10fl oz) pineapple juice
90ml (3fl oz) fresh lemon juice
60g (2oz) caster sugar
200g (7oz) pineapple pieces

Pour sauterne and juices into a chilled jug. Add sugar and pieces of pineapple. Stir well to dissolve sugar and refrigerate for two hours. Pour into chilled wine glasses until three-quarters full, then top up with champagne. Stir gently and serve.

BACARDI CHAMPAGNE PUNCH

MAKES 3.3L/111.58FL OZ | 13.5% ALC/VOL | 34.7 STANDARD DRINKS

1.5L (52fl oz) champagne
500ml (17fl oz) Bacardi
100ml (3⅓fl oz) amaretto
100ml (3⅓fl oz) Cointreau
50ml (1⅔fl oz) grenadine
50ml (1⅔fl oz) sugar syrup
1L (32fl oz) soda water
1 pineapple (peeled and cut into wedges)
8 frozen strawberries

Pour Bacardi, amaretto, Cointreau, grenadine and sugar into a chilled punch bowl then add wedges of pineapple. Stir and cover then refrigerate for two hours. Add soda and champagne then stir gently. Add strawberries and serve.

CHAMPAGNE PUNCH WITH MARASCHINO

MAKES 3.37L/113.95FL OZ | 14% ALC/VOL | 37.2 STANDARD DRINKS

3L (104fl oz) Brut Champagne
180ml (6fl oz) cognac
180ml (6fl oz) maraschino liqueur
5ml (1/6fl oz) orange bitters
2 fresh oranges (sliced thinly)
1 fresh lemon (sliced thinly)

Pour cognac, liqueur and bitters into a chilled punch bowl. Add slices of orange and lemon. Stir and refrigerate for one hour. Add a large block of ice and Champagne. Stir gently and serve.

NAVY PUNCH

MAKES 5.25L/177.52FL OZ | 10.3% ALC/VOL | 67.3 STANDARD DRINKS

4L (132fl oz) champagne
375ml (13fl oz) cognac
375ml (13fl oz) dark rum
375ml (13fl oz) peach brandy
120ml (4fl oz) fresh lemon juice
450g (15oz) caster sugar
4 pineapples (sliced)
Slices of lemon
Slices of orange
Slices of peach

Place sugar and slices of pineapple into a chilled punch bowl then mix well. Add cognac, rum, brandy and juice. Stir well and refrigerate to chill. Add slices of lemon, orange and peach. Add champagne, stir gently and serve.

CHAMPAGNE BLUES

MAKES 3.99L/134.91FL OZ | 13.5% ALC/VOL | 42.5 STANDARD DRINKS

3L (104fl oz) champagne
750ml (26fl oz) blue curaçao
240ml (8fl oz) fresh lemon juice
Peel of 2 fresh lemons (cut into strips)

Pour curaçao and juice into a punch bowl resting on a bed of ice. Stir well, add champagne and stir gently. Float lemon peel on top and serve.

DRAGOON PUNCH

MAKES 1.52L/51.39FL OZ | 11% ALC/VOL | 13.2 STANDARD DRINKS

750ml (26fl oz) champagne
250ml (8⅓fl oz) beer
250ml (8⅓fl oz) stout
90ml (3fl oz) brandy
90ml (3fl oz) sherry
90ml (3fl oz) sugar syrup
Slices of lemon

Pour beer, stout, brandy, sherry and sugar syrup into a jug over ice then add slices of lemon. Stir and add champagne. Stir gently and serve.

LAFAYETTE PUNCH

MAKES 4.75L/160.61FL OZ | 11.5% ALC/VOL | 45.4 STANDARD DRINKS

4L (132fl oz) champagne
750ml (26fl oz) moselle
1 cup caster sugar
6 fresh oranges (sliced)

Place slices of orange into a chilled punch bowl and cover with sugar. Add moselle and allow to stand for one hour. Add a large block of ice and champagne. Stir gently and serve.

CHAMPAGNE PUNCH
WITH KIRSCH

MAKES 3.9L/131.87FL OZ | 11.5% ALC/VOL | 35.4 STANDARD DRINKS

3L(104fl oz) champagne
150ml (5fl oz) kirsch
150ml (5fl oz) cream sherry
480ml (16fl oz) fresh orange juice
120ml (4fl oz) fresh lemon juice

Pour kirsch, sherry and juices into a punch bowl resting on a bed of ice. Stir and add champagne. Stir gently and serve.

PEACH CUP

MAKES 3.2L/108.20FL OZ | 12.6% ALC/VOL | 31.8 STANDARD DRINKS

1.5L (52fl oz) champagne
1.5L (52fl oz) dry white wine
105ml (3½fl oz) cognac
60ml (2fl oz) fresh lemon juice
30ml (1fl oz) sugar syrup
8 peach slices

Place peach slices into a chilled punch bowl then add cognac, juice and sugar syrup. Stir gently, cover and refrigerate for two hours. Add wine and stir well. Add champagne, stir gently and serve.

RUM

FISH HOUSE PUNCH

MAKES 1.3L/43.95FL OZ | 34% ALC/VOL | 34.2 STANDARD DRINKS

750ml (26fl oz) dark rum
375ml (13fl oz) brandy
60ml (2fl oz) peach brandy
60ml (2fl oz) sugar syrup
30ml (1fl oz) fresh lemon juice
Slices of lemon

Pour sugar syrup and juice into a mixing glass without ice. Stir well and pour into a punch bowl over a large block of ice. Add remaining ingredients, stir and serve.

ROMAN BOWL

MAKES 3.95L/133.56FL OZ | 19.5% ALC/VOL | 64.3 STANDARD DRINKS

1.5L (52fl oz) Bacardi
1.5L (52fl oz) champagne
325ml (11fl oz) peach brandy
375ml (13fl oz) pineapple juice
120ml (4fl oz) fresh lemon juice
120ml (4fl oz) fresh orange juice
120ml (4fl oz) sugar syrup
2 cups pineapple pieces
Strawberries

Pour Bacardi, brandy, juices and sugar syrup into a punch bowl over ice, then add pieces of pineapple. Stir and add champagne. Stir gently, add strawberries and serve.

BOOM BOOM PUNCH

MAKES 4.5L/152.16FL OZ | 21% ALC/VOL | 74.6 STANDARD DRINKS

2L (64fl oz) light rum
750ml (26fl oz) champagne
750ml (26fl oz) sweet vermouth
1L (32fl oz) fresh orange juice
Slices of banana

Pour rum, vermouth and juice into a punch bowl over a large block of ice. Stir, add champagne and stir gently. Add slices of banana and serve.

AVILLA

MAKES 0.5L./16.9FL OZ | 27.5% ALC/VOL | 10.7 STANDARD DRINKS

360ml (12fl oz) dark rum
15ml (½fl oz) peach brandy
90ml (3fl oz) fresh lime juice
30ml (1fl oz) honey

Pour ingredients into a blender over cracked ice and blend. Pour into chilled champagne saucers and serve.

CHAMPAGNE RUM PUNCH

MAKES 4.75L/160.61FL OZ | 20% ALC/VOL | 75 STANDARD DRINKS

1L (32fl oz) añejo rum
1L (32fl oz) light rum
750ml (26fl oz) champagne
750ml (26fl oz) sweet vermouth
1L (32fl oz) fresh orange juice
250ml (8⅓fl oz) cranberry juice
2 fresh oranges (sliced thinly)

Pour Rums, vermouth and juices into a chilled punch bowl. Stir well and add a large block of ice. Add champagne and stir gently. Add slices of orange and serve.

TIFFANY MARSHALL

MAKES 5.5L/185.97FL OZ | 13.1% ALC/VOL | 56.8 STANDARD DRINKS

1L (32fl oz) spiced rum
1L (32fl oz) vodka
500ml (17fl oz) fresh orange juice
3L (104fl oz) soda water
Slices of orange

Pour rum, vodka and juice into a punch bowl over a large block of ice. Stir well and add soda then stir gently. Add slices of orange and serve.

BRIDE'S BOWL

MAKES 5.31L/179.21FL OZ | 17.5% ALC/VOL | 73.3 STANDARD DRINKS

2.5L (78fl oz) Leilani Rum
500ml (17fl oz) pineapple juice
250ml (8⅓fl oz) fresh lemon juice
60ml (2fl oz) sugar syrup
2L (64fl oz) soda water
½ pineapple (sliced)
1 punnet strawberries (sliced)

Pour Rum, juices and sugar syrup into a chilled punch bowl then stir well. Refrigerate for one hour then add soda and stir gently. Add slices of pineapple and strawberries then serve.

BRUNCH PUNCH

MAKES 4.15L/140.32FL OZ | 9% ALC/VOL | 29.5 STANDARD DRINKS

1L (32fl oz) light rum
3L (104fl oz) tomato juice (chilled)
150ml (5fl oz) fresh lemon or lime juice
1½ teaspoons worcestershire sauce
Pinch of pepper
Pinch of salt
Slices of lemon or lime

Pour rum, juices and sauce into a punch bowl over a large block of ice. Add pepper and salt then stir. Add slices of lemon or lime as desired and serve.

VI'S JAMAICAN PUNCH

MAKES 5.36L/181.24FL OZ | 13.5% ALC/VOL | 58.4 STANDARD DRINKS

750ml (26fl oz) añejo rum
750ml (26fl oz) light rum
500ml (17fl oz) dark rum
1.5L (52fl oz) fresh orange juice
1L (32fl oz) pineapple juice
500ml (17fl oz) fresh lemon juice
360ml (12fl oz) soda water
½ cup caster sugar
1 teaspoon cinnamon (ground)
1 teaspoon nutmeg (grated)
½ teaspoon allspice
½ teaspoon mace
½ fresh pineapple (diced finely)
½ fresh pineapple (sliced thinly)

Pour lemon juice into a chilled punch bowl and add sugar. Stir well to dissolve sugar and add remaining ingredients then stir. Add a large block of ice and serve.

WHISTLER'S PUNCH

MAKES 2.11L/71.34FL OZ | 13% ALC/VOL | 21.7 STANDARD DRINKS

750ml (26fl oz) rum

3 dashes Angostura Bitters

1L (32fl oz) spring water

240ml (8fl oz) fresh lemon juice

120ml (4fl oz) sugar syrup

Nutmeg

Pour rum, Bitters, water, juice and sugar syrup into a punch bowl over ice. Stir well and serve in chilled old-fashioned glasses with nutmeg sprinkled over each serving.

GUAVA MILK PUNCH

MAKES 3.77L/127.47FL OZ | 11% ALC/VOL | 33.1 STANDARD DRINKS

750ml (26fl oz) light rum

180ml (6fl oz) golden rum

90ml (3fl oz) 151-proof rum

2.5L (78fl oz) fresh milk (chilled)

250ml (8⅓fl oz) fresh cream (chilled)

60g (2oz) sugar

12 twists of lemon peel

12 twists of orange peel

Pour rums, milk and cream into a chilled punch bowl then add sugar. Stir well to dissolve sugar then add a large block of ice and peels. Refrigerate for one hour then serve.

RUM CUP WITH WHITE WINE

MAKES 1.6L/54.10FL OZ | 22% ALC/VOL | 27.8 STANDARD DRINKS

750ml (26fl oz) light rum

300ml (10fl oz) dry white wine

60ml (2fl oz) Cointreau

60ml (2fl oz) falernum

250ml (8⅓fl oz) fresh orange juice

120ml (4fl oz) fresh lime juice

60ml (2fl oz) orgeat syrup

6 slices of lime

6 sprigs of fresh mint

Pour rum, wine, Cointreau, falernum, juices and syrup into a chilled jug. Add slices of lime and sprigs of mint. Stir well and refrigerate for two hours. Fill jug with ice, stir well and serve.

BLACK CHERRY RUM PUNCH

MAKES 2.13L/72.02FL OZ | 18.1% ALC/VOL | 30.4 STANDARD DRINKS

720ml (24fl oz) light rum

120ml (4fl oz) Crème De Cassis

120ml (4fl oz) dark rum

60ml (2fl oz) 151-proof Bacardi

240ml (8fl oz) sweet and sour mix

120ml (4fl oz) fresh orange juice

750ml (26fl oz) soda water

2 fresh limes (sliced thinly)

2 cans pitted black cherries

Pour rums, Cassis, Bacardi, sour mix and juice into a chilled punch bowl then stir. Refrigerate for one hour and add slices of lime. Add cherries and soda then stir gently. Place punch bowl on a bed of ice and serve.

AMBROSIA OF THE GODS

MAKES 1.32L/44.63FL OZ | 10.2% ALC/VOL | 10.6 STANDARD DRINKS

180ml (6fl oz) light rum
180ml (6fl oz) vodka
480ml (16fl oz) lemon-lime soda
480ml (16fl oz) orange soda

Pour rum and vodka into a jug over large amount of ice. Add sodas, stir gently and serve.

GIN & VODKA

GIN PUNCH

MAKES 1.59L/53.76FL OZ | 23.5% ALC/VOL | 29.5 STANDARD DRINKS

750ml (26fl oz) gin
125ml (4fl oz) brandy
125ml (4fl oz) Cointreau
90ml (3fl oz) fresh lemon juice
500ml (17fl oz) lemonade
Cucumber strips
Slices of lemon
Slices of orange

Pour gin, brandy, Cointreau and juice into a punch bowl over ice, then stir. Add remaining ingredients, stir gently and serve.

VODKA KNOCKOUT PUNCH

MAKES 2.4L/81.15FL OZ | 19% ALC/VOL | 36.1 STANDARD DRINKS

750ml (26fl oz) vodka
500ml (17fl oz) champagne
375ml (13fl oz) Midori
180ml (6fl oz) banana liqueur
600ml (20fl oz) fresh cream (chilled)
Slices of banana
Slices of melon
Strawberries

Pour vodka, Midori, liqueur and cream into a punch bowl over ice. Stir well then add slices of banana, melon and strawberries. Add champagne, stir gently and serve.

VODKA MILK PUNCH

10% ALC/VOL | 22.3 STANDARD DRINKS

This drink is a Milk Punch substituting Scotch Whisky with Vodka. See Milk Punch (page 188).

GIN MILK PUNCH

10% ALC/VOL | 22.3 STANDARD DRINKS

This drink is a Milk Punch substituting Scotch Whisky with Gin. See Milk Punch (page 188).

BACCIO

MAKES 1.01L/37.19FL OZ | 14.3% ALC/VOL | 11.4 STANDARD DRINKS

240ml (8fl oz) Calvert Gin
180ml (6fl oz) champagne
90ml (3fl oz) anisette
500ml (17fl oz) soda water
Slices of lemon
Slices of orange

Pour Gin and anisette into a jug over ice. Add slices of lemon and orange. Stir and add soda. Add champagne, stir gently and serve.

GIN PUNCH NO. 2

MAKES 5.84L/197.47FL OZ | 12.5% ALC/VOL | 57.6 STANDARD DRINKS

2L (64fl oz) gin
180ml (6fl oz) grenadine
1.8L (59fl oz) fresh orange juice
360ml (12fl oz) fresh lemon juice
1.5L (52fl oz) soda water

Pour gin, grenadine and juices into a chilled punch bowl. Stir well and add a large block of ice. Add soda, stir gently and serve.

JINX

MAKES 2.35L/79.46FL OZ | 13.1% ALC/VOL | 24.3 STANDARD DRINKS

600ml (20fl oz) vodka
300ml (10fl oz) blueberry schnapps
150ml (5fl oz) Bailey's Irish Cream
300ml (10fl oz) grape juice
1L (32fl oz) lemon-lime soda

Pour vodka, schnapps, Bailey's and juice into a punch bowl over a large block of ice. Stir well and add soda. Stir gently and serve.

EBOLA

MAKES 1.26L/42.60FL OZ | 27% ALC/VOL | 26.8 STANDARD DRINKS

180ml (6fl oz) vodka
180ml (6fl oz) blended whiskey
180ml (6fl oz) dark rum
180ml (6fl oz) gin
180ml (6fl oz) tequila
360ml (12fl oz) pineapple juice
Pinch of cinnamon

Pour vodka, whiskey, rum, gin, tequila and juice into a jug over crushed ice then add cinnamon. Stir well and serve.

ROD MUGGE

MAKES 1.40L/47.33FL OZ | 7% ALC/VOL | 7.8 STANDARD DRINKS

80ml (2⅔fl oz) vodka
80ml (2⅔fl oz) gin
80ml (2⅔fl oz) light rum
40ml (1⅓fl oz) Malibu
750ml (26fl oz) pink lemonade
375ml (13fl oz) lemon-lime soda

Pour vodka, gin, rum and Malibu into a cocktail shaker over ice. Shake and strain into a chilled jug. Add lemonade and soda. Stir gently and serve.

VODKA PUNCH

MAKES 1.10L/37.19FL OZ |28.5% ALC/VOL | 24.8 STANDARD DRINKS

750ml (26fl oz) vodka
90ml (3fl oz) Cointreau
250ml (8⅓fl oz) fresh orange juice
15ml (½fl oz) fresh lemon juice
Slices of lemon
Slices of orange

Pour vodka, Cointreau and juices into a punch bowl over ice. Add slices of lemon and orange. Stir well and serve.

MINTED GIN TEA

MAKES 0.50L/16.90FL OZ |4.4% ALC/VOL | 1.8 STANDARD DRINKS

60ml (2fl oz) gin
400ml (14fl oz) boiling water
30ml (1fl oz) fresh lemon juice
2 teaspoons fresh chopped mint
2 teaspoons black tea leaves
4 twists of lemon peel

Pour boiling water into a tea pot then add chopped mint and tea leaves. Allow to stand for five minutes to infuse then strain into a glass jug and refrigerate to chill. Add gin and juice then stir gently. Prepare four collins glasses with sugar-frosted rims. Pour minted tea into prepared glasses and garnish each serving with lemon peel.

WINE

QUINTET

MAKES 7.23L/244.47FL OZ | 6.5% ALC/VOL | 37.1 STANDARD DRINKS

3L (104fl oz) white wine
135ml (4½fl oz) brandy
135ml (4½fl oz) dark rum
720ml (24fl oz) fresh orange juice
240ml (8fl oz) fresh lemon juice
3L (104fl oz) soda water

Pour wine, brandy, rum and juices into a punch bowl over a large block of ice. Stir and add soda. Stir gently and serve.

RHINE WINE CUP

MAKES 0.84L/28.40FL OZ | 13.5% ALC/VOL | 9 STANDARD DRINKS

750ml (26fl oz) rhine riesling
60ml (2fl oz) maraschino liqueur
30ml (1fl oz) orange curaçao
1 teaspoon sugar syrup
Maraschino cherries
Slices of orange

Pour riesling, liqueur, curaçao and sugar syrup into a jug over ice. Add cherries and slices of orange. Stir and serve.

SAUTERNE CUP

MAKES 1.60L/54.10FL OZ | 12.5% ALC/VOL | 15.8 STANDARD DRINKS

1.5L (52fl oz) sauterne
30ml (1fl oz) brandy
30ml (1fl oz) orange curaçao
15ml (½fl oz) fresh lemon juice
15ml (½fl oz) fresh orange juice
15ml (½fl oz) sugar syrup
Slices of lemon
Slices of orange
Sprigs of fresh mint

Pour sauterne and sugar syrup into a mixing bowl without ice. Stir well and pour into a jug over ice. Add brandy, curaçao and juices whilst stirring. Add slices of lemon, orange and sprigs of mint then serve.

CLARET PUNCH NO. 2

MAKES 3.20L/108.20FL OZ | 6.6% ALC/VOL | 17.6 STANDARD DRINKS

1.5L (52fl oz) claret
68ml (2¼fl oz) cognac
68ml (2¼fl oz) curaçao
68ml (2¼fl oz) sherry
1.5L (52fl oz) soda water
225g (½lb) caster sugar
Rind of 1 fresh lemon

Pour claret into a mixing bowl without ice then add sugar and lemon rind. Stir well to dissolve sugar and refrigerate for three hours. Pour into a punch bowl over a large block of ice then add cognac, curaçao and sherry. Stir and add soda. Stir gently and serve.

WEDDING BELL PUNCH

MAKES 4.91L/166.02FL OZ | 13.5% ALC/VOL | 52.1 STANDARD DRINKS

2L (64fl oz) dry red wine
500ml (17fl oz) bourbon
360ml (12fl oz) añejo rum
240ml (8fl oz) sweet cermouth
190ml (6fl oz) champagne
120ml (4fl oz) Dark Crème De Cacao
500ml (17fl oz) fresh lemon juice
500ml (17fl oz) dry ginger ale
500ml (17fl oz) soda water
1 cup caster sugar
2 fresh oranges (sliced thinly)
1 punnet strawberries

Pour juice into a chilled punch bowl and add sugar, then stir well to dissolve sugar. Add wine, bourbon, rum, vermouth, cacao, ginger ale and soda. Stir and add a large block of ice. Add champagne and stir gently. Add slices of orange and strawberries then serve.

FLORENTINE PUNCH

MAKES 4.12L/139.31FL OZ | 18.9% ALC/VOL | 61.4 STANDARD DRINKS

1.5L (52fl oz) coffee cream marsala wine
1.5L (52fl oz) rosé wine
1L (32fl oz) brandy
120ml (4fl oz) fresh lemon juice
2 fresh oranges (sliced thinly in halves)

Pour wines, brandy and juice into a punch bowl over a large block of ice. Stir well and refrigerate for one hour. Float slices of orange on top and serve.

CARDINAL PUNCH

MAKES 5.34L/180.56FL OZ | 12% ALC/VOL | 50.4 STANDARD DRINKS

2L (64fl oz) claret
500ml (17fl oz) brandy
500ml (17fl oz) light rum
240ml (8fl oz) sweet vermouth
180ml (6fl oz) champagne
500ml (17fl oz) strong black tea (chilled)
360ml (12fl oz) fresh lemon juice
60ml (2fl oz) sugar syrup
1L (32fl oz) soda water
Slices of lemon
Slices of orange
Strawberries

Pour juice and sugar into a mixing glass without ice. Stir well and pour into a punch bowl over a large block of ice. Add claret, brandy, rum, vermouth and tea then stir. Add soda and champagne then stir gently. Add slices of lemon, orange and strawberries then serve.

GINGER PUNCH

MAKES 1.97L/66.61FL OZ | 6.5% ALC/VOL | 10.1 STANDARD DRINKS

700ml (24fl oz) dry white wine
120ml (4fl oz) golden rum
300ml (10fl oz) fresh orange juice
150ml (5fl oz) grapefruit juice
700ml (24fl oz) dry ginger ale

Pour wine, rum and juices into a jug without ice. Stir well and refrigerate for two hours. Add ginger ale, stir gently and serve.

MADEIRA PUNCH

MAKES 1.62L/1.62FL OZ | 8.5% ALC/VOL | 10.9 STANDARD DRINKS

750ml (26fl oz) medium dry Madeira
120ml (4fl oz) brandy
750ml (26fl oz) soda water
Slices of lemon
Slices of orange
Slices of peach
Strawberries

Pour Madeira and brandy into a jug over ice. Add slices of lemon, orange, peach and strawberries.
Stir and add soda. Stir gently and serve.

LOVING CUP

MAKES 0.79L/26.71FL OZ | 11.5% ALC/VOL | 7.2 STANDARD DRINKS

500ml (17fl oz) claret

60ml (2fl oz) brandy

30ml (1fl oz) Cointreau

20ml (⅔fl oz) sugar syrup

180ml (6fl oz) soda water

Cucumber rind

Slices of orange

Sprigs of fresh mint

Pour claret, brandy, Cointreau and sugar into a jug over ice then add slices of orange. Stir and add soda then stir gently. Place cucumber rind around rim of jug and add sprigs of mint then serve.

EMERALD BOWL

MAKES 4.21L/142.35FL OZ | 11% ALC/VOL | 36.5 STANDARD DRINKS

3L (104fl oz) emerald riesling (chilled)
180ml (6fl oz) apricot brandy
180ml (6fl oz) California brandy
850ml (29fl oz) apple juice
16 long slices of cucumber peel

Pour riesling, brandies and juice into a punch bowl over a large block of ice then add cucumber peel. Stir and refrigerate for one hour then serve.

FRANK DAVIS PUNCH

MAKES 5.74L/194.09FL OZ | 15.5% ALC/VOL | 71.7 STANDARD DRINKS

3L (104fl oz) sauterne
1.5L (52fl oz) champagne
1L (32fl oz) gold tequila
240ml (8fl oz) fresh lemon juice
½ cup caster sugar
1 honeydew melon (scooped into balls)

Pour juice into a chilled punch bowl and add sugar. Stir well to dissolve sugar then add sauterne, tequila and champagne. Stir gently and add a large block of ice. Add melon balls and serve.

RHINE WINE PUNCH

MAKES 4.70L/158.92FL OZ | 9% ALC/VOL | 33.4 STANDARD DRINKS

3L (104fl oz) rhine riesling

113ml (3¾fl oz) brandy

113ml (3¾fl oz) maraschino liqueur

250ml (8⅓fl oz) strong black tea (chilled)

225ml (7½fl oz) sugar syrup

1L (32fl oz) soda water

Slices of orange

Strawberries

Pour riesling, brandy, liqueur, tea and sugar syrup into a punch bowl resting on a bed of ice then stir well. Add soda, slices of orange and strawberries. Stir gently and serve.

PEACHES AND WINE

MAKES 1.50L/50.72FL OZ | 10% ALC/VOL | 14.1 STANDARD DRINKS

750ml (26fl oz) moselle (sparkling)

750ml (26fl oz) moselle (still)

1 tablespoon sugar syrup

3 fresh peaches (diced)

Place diced peaches into a punch bowl resting on a bed of ice and add half moselle (still) then allow to stand for half an hour to marinate. Add remaining ingredients, stir gently and serve when chilled.

TEQUILA PUNCH

MAKES 4.75L/160.61FL OZ | 17.5% ALC/VOL | 65.6 STANDARD DRINKS

3L (104fl oz) sauterne (chilled)
1L (32fl oz) tequila (chilled)
750ml (26fl oz) champagne
2kg (4½lb) fresh fruit (diced)

Pour sauterne and tequila into a punch bowl over ice then add diced fruit. Stir well and add champagne. Stir gently and serve.

CONFETTI PUNCH

MAKES 4.40L/148.78FL OZ | 10% ALC/VOL | 34.7 STANDARD DRINKS

1.5L (52fl oz) dry sparkling white wine
700ml (24fl oz) light rum
700ml (24fl oz) light grape juice
500ml (17fl oz) fresh orange juice
1L (32fl oz) lemonade
10 strawberries (halved)

Pour rum, juices and lemonade into a punch bowl over ice then stir. Add wine and strawberries.
Stir gently and serve.

STRAWBERRY PUNCH

MAKES 2.28L/77.09FL OZ | 11.5% ALC/VOL | 20.7 STANDARD DRINKS

700ml (24fl oz) red wine
700ml (24fl oz) sparkling white wine
200ml (6⅔fl oz) brandy
100ml (3⅓fl oz) strawberry liqueur
50ml (1⅔fl oz) strawberry syrup
30ml (1fl oz) fresh lemon juice
500ml (17fl oz) lemonade
Strawberries (sliced)

Pour red wine, brandy, liqueur, syrup and juice into a chilled punch bowl then stir. Add a large block of ice, lemonade, sliced strawberries and white wine. Stir gently and serve.

LIGHT WINE CUP

MAKES 1.31L/44.29FL OZ | 8.5% ALC/VOL | 8.8 STANDARD DRINKS

750ml (26fl oz) dry white wine
60ml (2fl oz) Galliano
2 dashes orange syrup/cordial
500ml (17fl oz) mineral water
Slices of orange

Pour wine, Galliano and syrup into a jug over ice then stir. Add mineral water and stir gently. Add slices of orange and serve.

SCORPION PUNCH

MAKES 1.18L/39.90FL OZ | 18% ALC/VOL | 16.8 STANDARD DRINKS

700ml (24fl oz) dry white wine

300ml (10fl oz) light rum

50ml (1⅔fl oz) brandy

50ml (1⅔fl oz) fresh orange juice

50ml (1⅔fl oz) fresh lemon juice

30ml (1fl oz) orgeat syrup

Slices of orange

Sprigs of fresh mint

Pour wine, rum, brandy, juices and syrup into a jug over ice. Add slices of orange and sprigs of mint. Stir and serve.

RED WINE PUNCH

MAKES 3.28L/110.90FL OZ | 12% ALC/VOL | 31.1 STANDARD DRINKS

1.5L (52fl oz) red wine

750ml (26fl oz) port

375ml (13fl oz) cherry brandy

450ml (15fl oz) fresh orange juice

120ml (4fl oz) sugar syrup

90ml (3fl oz) fresh lemon juice

Maraschino cherries

Slices of lemon

Slices of orange

Pour wine, port, brandy, juices and sugar syrup into a punch bowl over ice then add remaining ingredients. Stir and add soda water to taste, if desired. Stir gently then serve.

ROSÉ PUNCH

MAKES 4.23L/143.03FL OZ | 8.5% ALC/VOL | 28.4 STANDARD DRINKS

3L (104fl oz) rosé wine (chilled)
540ml (18fl oz) cranberry liqueur
120ml (4fl oz) california brandy
570ml (19fl oz) soda water
16 thin pineapple slices
1 punnet strawberries

Pour wine, liqueur and brandy into a punch bowl over a large block of ice. Add pineapple slices and strawberries. Stir and refrigerate for one hour. Add soda, stir gently and serve.

SAUTERNES FISH HOUSE PUNCH

MAKES 1.71L/57.82FL OZ | 12% ALC/VOL | 16.2 STANDARD DRINKS

1.5L (52fl oz) sauterne
30ml (1fl oz) dry orange curaçao
30ml (1fl oz) Grand Marnier
30ml (1fl oz) maraschino liqueur
120ml (4fl oz) sugar syrup
Slices of orange
Strawberries

Pour sauterne, curaçao, Grand Marnier, liqueur and sugar into a jug over ice. Add slices of orange and strawberries. Stir well and serve.

BOATMAN'S CUP

MAKES 2.36L/79.80FL OZ | 5.5% ALC/VOL | 10.1 STANDARD DRINKS

700ml (24fl oz) dry white wine
500ml (17fl oz) dry cider
60ml (2fl oz) brandy
400ml (14fl oz) fresh orange juice
700ml (24fl oz) lemonade
1 fresh orange (sliced in halves)
20 melon (scooped into balls)

Pour wine, brandy and juice into a chilled punch bowl. Stir and refrigerate for three hours. Add lemonade, slices of orange and melon balls then stir gently. Add cider, stir gently and serve.

LYCHEE PUNCH BOWL

MAKES 2.38L/80.47FL OZ | 7.9% ALC/VOL | 19.3 STANDARD DRINKS

1.5L (52fl oz) dry white wine
700ml (24fl oz) dry cider
150ml (5fl oz) dry sherry
15ml (½fl oz) maraschino liqueur
15ml (½fl oz) fresh lemon juice
900g (2lb) canned lychees

Pour 750ml (26fl oz) wine, sherry, liqueur and juice into a chilled punch bowl then add lychees. Stir and refrigerate for two hours. Add remaining 750ml (26fl oz) wine and the cider. Stir gently and serve.

FOURTH OF JULY PUNCH

MAKES 4.84L/163.65FL OZ | 11.4% ALC/VOL | 50.3 STANDARD DRINKS

2.25L (72fl oz) red wine (chilled)
750ml (26fl oz) brandy
750ml (26fl oz) champagne
720ml (24fl oz) fresh lemon juice
375ml (13fl oz) strong black tea (chilled)
1kg (2lb 4oz) caster sugar
Slices of lemon

Pour juice into a chilled punch bowl and add sugar. Stir well to dissolve sugar and fill bowl with ice. Add wine, brandy and tea. Stir and add champagne then stir gently. Serve in chilled goblets with a slice of lemon as garnish for each serving.

PINEAPPLE PUNCH

MAKES 2.72L/91.97FL OZ | 7.5% ALC/VOL | 16.1 STANDARD DRINKS

1.5L (52fl oz) oselle
30ml (1fl oz) gin
30ml (1fl oz) maraschino liqueur
5ml (1/6fl oz) Angostura Bitters
30ml (1fl oz) grenadine
90ml (3fl oz) fresh lemon juice
30ml (1fl oz) pine syrup/cordial
1L (32fl oz) soda water
½ fresh lemon (sliced)
Slices of pineapple

Pour moselle, gin, liqueur, Bitters, grenadine, juice and syrup into a punch bowl resting on a bed of ice then stir well. Add soda and stir gently. Add slices of lemon and pineapple. Stir gently and serve.

MOSELLE BOWL

MAKES 3.96L/133.90FL OZ | 17% ALC/VOL | 53.2 STANDARD DRINKS

3L (104fl oz) moselle
480ml (16fl oz) brandy
360ml (12fl oz) Grand Marnier
125ml (4fl oz) sugar syrup
1 pineapple (peeled and sliced thinly)
1 punnet strawberries (cut into halves)

Pour brandy, Grand Marnier and sugar syrup into a mixing bowl without ice then add slices of pineapple. Stir gently and refrigerate for 24 hours. Pour moselle into a punch bowl over a large block of ice and add pre-chilled mixture. Stir and refrigerate for 30 minutes. Add strawberries and serve.

APPLE CUP

MAKES 3.05L/103.13FL OZ | 11.8% ALC/VOL | 28.3 STANDARD DRINKS

2.25L (72fl oz) white wine
750ml (26fl oz) champagne
45ml (1½fl oz) sugar syrup
4 apples (peeled and diced)
1 lemon
Pinch of cinnamon

Place diced apple into a chilled punch bowl and peel lemon in a long single spiral then juice the lemon. Pour juice into bowl over diced apple then add sugar syrup, lemon peel and cinnamon. Add 750ml (26fl oz) of wine and stir gently. Cover and refrigerate for six hours. Add remainder of wine and champagne. Stir gently and serve.

BANANA CUP

MAKES 3.85L/130.18FL OZ | 12.1% ALC/VOL | 37.5 STANDARD DRINKS

2.25L (72fl oz) white wine
1.5L (52fl oz) champagne
45ml (1½fl oz) light rum
23ml (¾fl oz) maraschino liqueur
30ml (1fl oz) fresh lemon juice
6 bananas (sliced)
5 tablespoons sugar

Place slices of banana into a chilled punch bowl then add rum, liqueur, juice and sugar. Stir well and add 750ml (26fl oz) wine. Stir, cover and refrigerate for two hours. Add remaining wine and stir. Add champagne, stir gently and serve.

APPLE-CALVADOS BOWL

MAKES 3.13L/105.83FL OZ | 9.8% ALC/VOL | 24.5 STANDARD DRINKS

1.5L (52fl oz) white wine
750ml (26fl oz) champagne
105ml (3½fl oz) Calvados
750ml (26fl oz) mineral water
30ml (1fl oz) fresh lemon juice
2 tablespoons sugar
8 wedges of apple

Place wedges of apple into a chilled punch bowl and pour juice over apple. Sprinkle sugar on top, cover and refrigerate for four hours. Add wine and Calvados then stir well. Add champagne and mineral water. Stir gently and serve.

MOUNTAIN ATTITUDE PUNCH

MAKES 3.54L/119.70FL OZ | 12.1% ALC/VOL | 33.8 STANDARD DRINKS

2.25L (72fl oz) red wine
180ml (6fl oz) amaretto
180ml (6fl oz) brandy
180ml (6fl oz) cherry brandy
750ml (26fl oz) dry ginger ale

Pour wine, amaretto and brandies into a punch bowl over ice. Stir and add ginger ale. Stir gently and serve.

BLACKBERRY CUP

MAKES 3.07L/103.80FL OZ | 12.4% ALC/VOL | 30.1 STANDARD DRINKS

2.25L (72fl oz) white wine
750ml (26fl oz) champagne
45ml (1½fl oz) orange curaçao
23ml (¾fl oz) light rum
1½ teaspoons sugar syrup
450g (1lb) blackberries

Pour curaçao, rum and sugar syrup into a chilled punch bowl then add blackberries. Stir gently and refrigerate for one hour. Add wine and champagne. Stir gently and place punch bowl on a bed of ice then serve.

COLD DUCK

MAKES 4.5L/151.16FL OZ | 12% ALC/VOL | 42.6 STANDARD DRINKS

3L (104fl oz) white wine
1.5L (52fl oz) champagne
Peel of 2 lemons

Place lemon peels into a punch bowl resting on a bed of ice and add wine. Add champagne and stir gently. Allow to stand for five minutes then remove peels from punch and serve.

BERRY PUNCH

MAKES 3.21L/108.54FL OZ | 12.4% ALC/VOL | 31.4 STANDARD DRINKS

2.25L (72fl oz) rosé wine
750ml (26fl oz) champagne
210ml (7fl oz) cream sherry
2 teaspoons sugar
450g (1lb) strawberries (halves)
225g (½lb) blackberries (halves)
225g (½lb) raspberries (halves)

Place berries into a chilled punch bowl and sprinkle sugar on top. Refrigerate for 20 minutes then add sherry, cover and refrigerate for one hour. Add wine and stir. Add champagne, stir gently and serve.

BRANDY

BRANDY PUNCH

MAKES 3.12L/105.49FL OZ | 20% ALC/VOL | 49.2 STANDARD DRINKS

1.5L (52fl oz) brandy
250ml (8⅓fl oz) curaçao
60ml (2fl oz) grenadine
500ml (17fl oz) sugar syrup
450ml (15fl oz) fresh lemon juice
360ml (12fl oz) fresh orange juice
Slices of lemon
Slices of orange

Pour brandy, curaçao, grenadine, sugar syrup and juices into a punch bowl over ice. Add slices of lemon and orange. Stir well and serve.

AMERICAN PUNCH

MAKES 1.47L/49.70FL OZ | 12.5% ALC/VOL | 15.7 STANDARD DRINKS

360ml (12fl oz) cherry brandy
180ml (6fl oz) blue curaçao
180ml (6fl oz) bourbon
750ml (26fl oz) lemonade
4 scoops vanilla ice-cream

Place ice-cream in centre of a punch bowl and surround ice-cream with ice. Pour bourbon over the ice and layer brandy on top. Add curaçao by pouring over the brandy and gently add lemonade—do not stir, then serve.

BRANDY CRUSTA PUNCH

MAKES 1.51L/51.05FL OZ | 23% ALC/VOL | 27.4 STANDARD DRINKS

750ml (26fl oz) brandy
250ml (8⅓fl oz) orange curaçao
10ml (⅓fl oz) Angostura Bitters
500ml (17fl oz) fresh orange juice

Prepare a punch bowl with a sugar-frosted rim and add ice. Pour ingredients into a mixing bowl without ice and stir well. Pour into prepared bowl and serve.

CHAMPS ELYSEES PUNCH

MAKES 0.45L/15.21FL OZ | 29% ALC/VOL | 8.3 STANDARD DRINKS

270ml (9fl oz) cognac
90ml (3fl oz) Yellow Chartreuse
Dash Angostura Bitters
90ml (3fl oz) fresh lemon juice
2 teaspoons sugar syrup

Pour ingredients into a blender over cracked ice and blend. Strain into four chilled cocktail glasses and serve.

BRANDY ALEXANDER PUNCH

MAKES 2.62L/88.59FL OZ | 14% ALC/VOL | 29 STANDARD DRINKS

750ml (26fl oz) brandy
375ml (13fl oz) Dark Crème De Cacao
1.5L (52fl oz) thick cream (chilled)
Green and red maraschino cherries
Nutmeg

Pour brandy, Cacao and cream into a punch bowl over ice. Stir until ingredients begin to thicken then sprinkle nutmeg on top. Add cherries and serve.

APPLE GINGER PUNCH

MAKES 4.12L/139.31FL OZ | 10.5% ALC/VOL | 34.6 STANDARD DRINKS

750ml (26fl oz) applejack
750ml (26fl oz) Green Ginger Wine
60ml (2fl oz) kirsch
60ml (2fl oz) maraschino liqueur
1.5L (52fl oz) ginger beer
1L (32fl oz) pineapple-grapefruit juice
2 red apples (cut into wedges, unpeeled)
2 yellow apples (cut into wedges, unpeeled)

Pour applejack, wine, kirsch, liqueur and juice into a punch bowl over a large block of ice. Stir and refrigerate for one hour. Add ginger beer and stir gently. Float wedges of apple on top and serve.

BRANDY EGG NOG BOWL

MAKES 4.11L/138.97FL OZ | 7.3% ALC/VOL | 27.3 STANDARD DRINKS

750ml (26fl oz) cognac
120ml (4fl oz) Jamaica rum
3L (104fl oz) fresh milk (chilled)
240ml (8fl oz) thick cream (chilled)
125g (4½oz) sugar
12 fresh eggs
Nutmeg

Separate eggs; pour egg yolks into a mixing bowl and add sugar. Beat well and pour into a chilled punch bowl. Add cognac, rum, milk and cream. Beat well and refrigerate for two hours. Pour egg whites into a clean mixing bowl and beat until stiff just prior to serving. Fold whites into punch until thoroughly blended and sprinkle nutmeg on top then serve.

SWEDISH PUNCH

MAKES 1L/33.81FL OZ | 29.5% ALC/VOL | 29.1 STANDARD DRINKS

500ml (17fl oz) brandy

500ml (17fl oz) rum

1 cup almonds

1 cup sugar

½ cup raisins

12 cardamom seeds

10 whole cloves

3 cinnamon sticks (crushed)

Rind of 1 fresh orange

Pour brandy and rum into a saucepan then add remaining ingredients. Slowly heat to the boil, stirring occasionally then remove from heat and allow to cool to room temperature. Refrigerate to chill then strain into a chilled jug and serve.

XALAPA PUNCH

MAKES 5.32L/179.89FL OZ | 12.5% ALC/VOL | 52.5 STANDARD DRINKS

750ml (26fl oz) applejack

750ml (26fl oz) claret

750ml (26fl oz) golden rum

2.5L (78fl oz) hot, strong black tea

570ml (19fl oz) sugar syrup

1 fresh lemon (sliced thinly)

Peel of 2 fresh lemons (grated)

Pour hot tea into a punch bowl over a silver spoon (to prevent bowl cracking) and add grated lemon peel. Stir and allow to stand for fifteen minutes then refrigerate to chill. Add ice and remaining ingredients. Stir well and serve.

APPLE EGG PUNCH

MAKES 4.39L/148.44FL OZ | 8% ALC/VOL | 31.9 STANDARD DRINKS

1L (32fl oz) applejack
3L (104fl oz) fresh milk (chilled)
375ml (13fl oz) thick cream (chilled)
15ml (½fl oz) vanilla extract
½ cup sugar
12 fresh eggs
Cinnamon

Place sugar and eggs into a blender without ice. Blend and pour into a chilled punch bowl. Add applejack and beat to blend. Add milk, cream and extract. Stir well and refrigerate for one hour. Sprinkle cinnamon on top and serve.

APPLEJACK PUNCH

MAKES 2.19L/74.05FL OZ | 13.5% ALC/VOL | 23.3 STANDARD DRINKS

750ml (26fl oz) applejack
90ml (3fl oz) grenadine
300ml (10fl oz) fresh lemon juice
300ml (10fl oz) fresh orange juice
750ml (26fl oz) dry ginger ale
Slices of apple
Sprigs of fresh mint

Pour applejack, grenadine and juices into a punch bowl over ice. Add slices of apple and sprigs of mint. Stir well and add ginger ale. Stir gently and serve.

AMBASSADOR'S MORNING LIFT

MAKES 1.36L/45.98FL OZ | 9.3% ALC/VOL | 10 STANDARD DRINKS

180ml (6fl oz) cognac*

90ml (3fl oz) light rum

90ml (3fl oz) White Crème De Cacao

1L (32fl oz) dairy egg nog (see recipe page 23)

nutmeg

* Bourbon or brandy may substitute cognac if desired.

Pour Cognac, Rum, Cacao and egg nog into a chilled jug. Stir well and sprinkle nutmeg over each serving.

IRISH APPLE BOWL

MAKES 4.13L/139.65FL OZ | 12% ALC/VOL | 38.8 STANDARD DRINKS

750ml (26fl oz) applejack
480ml (16fl oz) blended irish whiskey
300ml (10fl oz) Rose's lime juice
2.6L (80fl oz) dry ginger ale
4 fresh limes (sliced thinly)
2 red apples (diced)

Pour applejack, whiskey and juice into a punch bowl over a large block ice. Add slices of lime and diced apple. Stir and refrigerate for one hour. Add ginger ale, stir gently and serve.

WHISKEY

ARTILLERY PUNCH

MAKES 4.06L/137.28FL OZ | 19% ALC/VOL | 60.9 STANDARD DRINKS

750ml (26fl oz) Canadian whisky
750ml (26fl oz) claret
500ml (17fl oz) golden rum
250ml (8⅓fl oz) cognac
250ml (8⅓fl oz) gin
60ml (2fl oz) Bénédictine
750ml (26fl oz) strong black tea (chilled)
500ml (17fl oz) fresh orange juice
250ml (8⅓fl oz) fresh lemon juice
Slices of lemon
Slices of orange

Pour whisky, claret, rum, cognac, gin, Bénédictine, tea and juices into a punch bowl over ice. Add slices of lemon and orange. Stir and serve.

BOURBON MILK PUNCH

10.5% ALC/VOL | 23.4 STANDARD DRINKS

This drink is a Milk Punch substituting Scotch whisky with bourbon and adding sugar syrup if desired.
See Milk Punch (page 188).

WHISKY PUNCH

MAKES 2.64L/89.26FL OZ | 17.5% ALC/VOL | 36.5 STANDARD DRINKS

1.125L (38fl oz) Scotch whisky

60ml (2fl oz) curaçao

30ml (1fl oz) grenadine

500ml (17fl oz) apple juice

180ml (6fl oz) fresh lemon juice

750ml (26fl oz) dry ginger ale or soda water

Diced apple

Slices of lemon

Slices of orange

Pour whisky, curaçao, grenadine and juices into a punch bowl over ice. Add diced apple, slices of lemon and orange. Stir and add ginger ale or soda as desired. Stir gently and serve.

BERMUDA BOURBON PUNCH

MAKES 3.64L/123.08FL OZ | 9.1% ALC/VOL | 28.3 STANDARD DRINKS

750ml (26fl oz) bourbon

240ml (8fl oz) Madeira

120ml (4fl oz) falernum

45ml (1½fl oz) Pernod

750ml (26fl oz) boiling water

240ml (8fl oz) fresh lemon juice

1.5L (52fl oz) dry ginger ale

3 tablespoons jasmine tea leaves

3 fresh lemons (sliced thinly)

Spiced walnuts

Pour boiling water into a container and add tea leaves then allow to stand for five minutes. Strain into a jug and allow to cool to room temperature then refrigerate to chill. Pour into a punch bowl over a large block of ice then add bourbon, Madeira, falernum, Pernod and juice. Stir well and refrigerate for one hour. Add ginger ale and slices of lemon then stir gently. Add a spiced walnut to each serving.

MINT JULEP PUNCH

MAKES 5.19L/175.49FL OZ | 6% ALC/VOL | 25.8 STANDARD DRINKS

820ml (28fl oz) bourbon

1.5L (52fl oz) pineapple juice

1L (32fl oz) spring water

120ml (4fl oz) fresh lime juice

1.75L (58fl oz) lemon-lime soda

1 cup set mint jelly (made from jelly crystals)

Slices of lime

Sprigs of fresh mint

Pour 500ml (17fl oz) water into a saucepan and add jelly. Heat slowly stirring continuously to melt jelly then remove from heat and allow to cool. Add bourbon, juices and remaining 500ml (17fl oz) water. Stir and refrigerate to chill. Pour into a punch bowl over a large block of ice and add soda then stir gently. Add slices of lime and sprigs of mint then serve.

ARTILLERYMAN'S PUNCH

MAKES 3.71L/125.45FL OZ | 16% ALC/VOL | 46.8 STANDARD DRINKS

1L (32fl oz) bourbon
270ml (9fl oz) light rum
180ml (6fl oz) apricot brandy
120ml (4fl oz) dark Jamaica rum
1L (32fl oz) strong black tea (chilled)
720ml (24fl oz) fresh orange juice
360ml (12fl oz) fresh lemon juice
60ml (2fl oz) sugar syrup

Pour ingredients into a punch bowl over a large block of ice, stir well and serve.

MILK PUNCH

MAKES 2.83L/95.69FL OZ | 10.5% ALC/VOL | 23.4 STANDARD DRINKS

750ml (26fl oz) Scotch whisky
2L (64fl oz) fresh milk (chilled)
80ml (2⅔fl oz) sugar syrup
Nutmeg

Pour whisky, milk and sugar into a punch bowl over ice, then stir. Sprinkle nutmeg on top and serve.

CHRISTMAS YULE EGG NOG

MAKES 1.40L/47.33FL OZ | 11.4% ALC/VOL | 12.6 STANDARD DRINKS

360ml (12fl oz) Scotch whisky
45ml (1½fl oz) light rum
1L (32fl oz) dairy egg nog (see recipe page 23)
Nutmeg

Pour whisky, rum and egg nog into a punch bowl resting on a bed of ice. Stir well and sprinkle nutmeg over each serving.

NASHVILLE EGG NOG

MAKES 1.36L/45.98FL OZ | 10.2% ALC/VOL | 10.9 STANDARD DRINKS

180ml (6fl oz) bourbon
90ml (3fl oz) brandy
90ml (3fl oz) light rum
1L (32fl oz) dairy egg nog (see recipe page 23)
Nutmeg

Pour bourbon, brandy, rum and egg nog into a punch bowl over a large block of ice. Stir well and sprinkle nutmeg over each serving.

ALL-AMERICAN NOG

MAKES 2.48L/83.85FL OZ | 6.8% ALC/VOL | 14.6 STANDARD DRINKS

240ml (8fl oz) bourbon
240ml (8fl oz) Puerto Rican rum
2L (64fl oz) dairy egg nog (see recipe page 23)
8 x 150ml (5fl oz) vanilla ice-cream (shaped into balls/cups)

Pour bourbon, rum and egg nog into a chilled punch bowl then stir well. Float ice-cream balls in punch bowl then add a teaspoon of ice-cream to each serving.

CIDER

SOMERSET PUNCH

MAKES 1.87L/63.23FL OZ | 5% ALC/VOL | 7.4 STANDARD DRINKS

1L (32fl oz) dry cider
150ml (5fl oz) dry white wine
60ml (2fl oz) apple brandy
150ml (5fl oz) apple juice
150ml (5fl oz) fresh orange juice
60ml (2fl oz) fresh lemon juice
300ml (10fl oz) dry ginger ale
Strawberries (sliced)

Pour cider, wine, brandy and juices into a punch bowl over a large block of ice. Stir and add ginger ale. Add sliced strawberries, stir gently and serve.

KNOCKOUT PUNCH

MAKES 1.42L/48.01FL OZ | 6% ALC/VOL | 6.7 STANDARD DRINKS

1L (32fl oz) cider
30ml (1fl oz) Bénédictine
30ml (1fl oz) brandy
30ml (1fl oz) gin
30ml (1fl oz) peach brandy
300ml (10fl oz) Lemonade

Pour cider, Bénédictine, brandies and gin into a jug. Stir and refrigerate for two hours. Add lemonade, stir gently and serve.

CIDER CUP

MAKES 1.82L/61.54FL OZ | 5% ALC/VOL | 5.2 STANDARD DRINKS

1.5L (52fl oz) cider (chilled)
30ml (1fl oz) brandy
30ml (1fl oz) orange curaçao
200ml (6⅔fl oz) fresh orange juice
60ml (2fl oz) fresh lemon juice
Slices of lemon
Slices of orange

Pour brandy, curaçao and juices into a jug over ice. Add slices of lemon and orange. Add cider, stir gently and serve.

TUVE NIGHTMARE

MAKES 10L/338.14FL OZ | 9.1% ALC/VOL | 71.8 STANDARD DRINKS

5L (165fl oz) cider
1.5L (52fl oz) vodka
500ml (17fl oz) Pisang Ambon
1.5L (52fl oz) dry ginger ale
1.5L (52fl oz) lemonade
Slices of cucumber
Slices of lime

Pour vodka into a punch bowl over ice and add Cider. Add slices of cucumber and lime. Add ginger ale and lemonade then stir gently. Add Pisang Ambon, stir and serve.

CIDER FIZZ

MAKES 1.58L/53.42FL OZ | 4.1% ALC/VOL | 6.3 STANDARD DRINKS

1L (32fl oz) cider
90ml (3fl oz) rum
360ml (12fl oz) fresh orange juice
120ml (4fl oz) fresh lemon juice
15ml (½fl oz) spring water
350g (12oz) caster sugar
2 tablespoons icing sugar
White of 3 eggs
Pinch of salt

Pour cider into a saucepan and add caster sugar then gently heat to a simmer whilst stirring frequently. Remove from heat and refrigerate to cool. Pour into a chilled jug then add rum and juices. Stir and refrigerate for one hour. Pour water and egg whites into a mixing bowl then add salt. Beat well and add icing sugar then beat again. Pour cider mixture into bowl over egg white mixture and beat. Pour combined mixtures into a clean chilled jug and serve.

SANGRIA

SANGRIA

MAKES 1.29L/43.62FL OZ | 10.5% ALC/VOL | 10.7 STANDARD DRINKS

750ml (26fl oz) red wine
120ml (4fl oz) brandy
50ml (1⅔fl oz) sugar syrup
375ml (13fl oz) soda water
Slices of lemon
Slices of lime
Slices of orange

Pour wine, brandy and sugar into a jug over ice. Add slices of lemon, lime and orange then stir. Add soda, stir gently and serve.

BAYLOR SANGRIA

MAKES 11L/371.95FL OZ | 9% ALC/VOL | 78.1 STANDARD DRINKS

6L (195fl oz) red wine
750ml (26fl oz) brandy
4L (132fl oz) tropical fruit juice
250ml (8⅓fl oz) sugar syrup
Slices of fresh fruit

Pour wine, brandy, juice and sugar syrup into a chilled punch bowl. Stir well and refrigerate to chill. Add slices of fruit and place punch bowl on a bed of ice then serve.

SANGRIA ESPECIALE

MAKES 2.65L/89.60FL OZ | 13.2% ALC/VOL | 28.7 STANDARD DRINKS

1.5L (52fl oz) red wine
750ml (26fl oz) champagne
120ml (4fl oz) cognac
120ml (4fl oz) gin
90ml (3fl oz) fresh orange juice
75ml (2½fl oz) fresh lemon juice
½ cup caster sugar
Slices of lemon
Slices of orange

Pour wine, cognac, gin and juices into a punch bowl over ice then add sugar. Stir well and add champagne then stir gently. Add slices of lemon and orange then serve.

VARIOUS

TEXAS BAR PUNCH

MAKES 3.5L/ 118.34 | 7.7% ALC/VOL | 21.3 STANDARD DRINKS

1.5L (52fl oz) ruby port
1L (32fl oz) dry ginger ale
1L (32fl oz) lemon-lime soda
1 fresh lemon (sliced)
1 fresh orange (sliced)

Pour port, ginger ale and soda into a chilled punch bowl. Stir gently and add a large block of ice. Add slices of lemon and orange then serve.

MIDORI PUNCH

MAKES 2.25L/76.08FL OZ | 19.5% ALC/VOL | 34.6 STANDARD DRINKS

750ml (26fl oz) Midori
750ml (26fl oz) vodka
750ml (26fl oz) lemonade
Slices of lemon
Slices of orange

Pour Midori and Vodka into a punch bowl over ice. Add slices of lemon and orange. Stir and add lemonade. Stir gently and serve.

CHOCOLATE PUNCH

MAKES 1.37L/46.32FL OZ | 4.5% ALC/VOL | 4.9 STANDARD DRINKS

375ml (13fl oz) Bailey's Irish Cream
1L (32fl oz) fresh milk (chilled)
Nutmeg

Pour Bailey's and milk into a blender over crushed ice. Blend until smooth and pour into a chilled jug then serve with nutmeg lightly sprinkled over each serving.

CHOCOLATE COCKTAIL PUNCH

MAKES 0.24L/8.11FL OZ | 19% ALC/VOL | 4.5 STANDARD DRINKS

180ml (6fl oz) port
60ml (2fl oz) Yellow Chartreuse
Yolk of 4 eggs
4 teaspoons dark chocolate (grated)
Slices of kiwi fruit

Pour port, Chartreuse and egg yolks into a blender over cracked ice then add grated chocolate. Blend and strain into a jug. Pour into chilled cocktail glasses and garnish with a slice of kiwi fruit with each serving.

EL GRITO

MAKES 1.52L/51.39FL OZ | 17.5% ALC/VOL | 21 STANDARD DRINKS

700ml (24fl oz) gold tequila
700ml (24fl oz) strawberry purée
120ml (4fl oz) sugar syrup
6 strawberries (diced)

Pour tequila and sugar syrup into a jug over crushed ice. Add puréed and diced strawberries. Stir well to combine all ingredients and serve.

MEXICAN TEA PUNCH

MAKES 1.5L/50.72FL OZ | 12.9% ALC/VOL | 15.2 STANDARD DRINKS

500ml (17fl oz) tequila
8ml (¼fl oz) Angostura Bitters
500ml (17fl oz) strong black tea (chilled)
250ml (8⅓fl oz) pineapple juice
60ml (2fl oz) fresh lemon juice
60ml (2fl oz) fresh lime juice
60ml (2fl oz) honey
60ml (2fl oz) spring water
1½ teaspoons cinnamon

Pour tequila, Bitters, tea, juices, honey and water into a chilled jug then add cinnamon. Stir well and refrigerate to chill. Add ice, stir and serve.

RUN AND GO NAKED

MAKES 6L/202.88FL OZ | 8.4% ALC/VOL | 39.8 STANDARD DRINKS

4.5L (150fl oz) beer
750ml (26fl oz) vodka (chilled)
750ml (26fl oz) lemonade concentrate

Pour beer into a chilled punch bowl and add vodka. Add concentrate, stir gently and serve.

MALIBU TEQUICHI PUNCH

MAKES 4.25L/143.70FL OZ | 17.6% ALC/VOL | 59 STANDARD DRINKS

1.75L (58fl oz) Malibu
1L (32fl oz) tequila
1.5L (52fl oz) pineapple juice
Slices of pineapple

Pour Malibu, Tequila and juice into a punch bowl over a large block of ice then stir well. Add slices of pineapple and serve.

MALIBLUE LAGOON PUNCH

MAKES 4.75L/160.61FL OZ | 13% ALC/VOL | 48.7 STANDARD DRINKS

1.75L (58fl oz) Malibu
1L (32fl oz) blue curaçao
2L (64fl oz) soda water
Cherries
Slices of orange

Pour Malibu and curaçao into a punch bowl over a large block of ice. Add soda and stir gently. Add cherries and slices of orange then serve.

MALIBU MIMOSA PUNCH

MAKES 4.25L/143.70FL OZ | 11.5% ALC/VOL | 38.6 STANDARD DRINKS

1.75L (58fl oz) Malibu
1L (32fl oz) champagne
1.5L (52fl oz) fresh orange juice
Slices of orange

Pour Malibu and juice into a punch bowl over a large block of ice then stir. Add champagne and stir gently. Add slices of orange and serve.

HOT
TEMPTATIONS

GLÖGG

MAKES 2L/67.62FL OZ | 18% ALC/VOL | 28.4 STANDARD DRINKS

750ml (26fl oz) red wine
750ml (26fl oz) medium sherry
375ml (13fl oz) brandy
8ml (¼fl oz) Angostura Bitters
120ml (4fl oz) sugar syrup
Almonds
Raisins

Pour wine, sherry, brandy, Bitters and sugar syrup into a saucepan then heat to a simmer without boiling whilst stirring frequently. Remove from heat and pour into pre-warmed beer mugs that contain an almond and raisin; pour over a silver spoon (to prevent mugs cracking) then serve.

COFFEE-PORT PUNCH

MAKES 0.75L/25.36FL OZ | 18.3% ALC/VOL | 10.8 STANDARD DRINKS

250ml (8⅓fl oz) dark rum
250ml (8⅓fl oz) white port
250ml (8⅓fl oz) hot black coffee
Sugar to taste

Pour rum, port and coffee into a saucepan. Heat to drinking temperature without boiling whilst stirring occasionally then add sugar to taste and stir to dissolve sugar. Remove from heat and pour into coffee glasses over a silver spoon (to prevent glasses cracking) then serve.

FESTIVAL PUNCH

MAKES 2L/67.62FL OZ | 20.5% ALC/VOL | 32.9 STANDARD DRINKS

1L (32fl oz) Jamaica rum

1L (32fl oz) sweet apple cider

1½ tablespoons butter

2 cinnamon sticks (crushed)

Pour rum and cider into a saucepan. Add butter and cinnamon. Heat to boiling point without boiling whilst stirring frequently then remove from heat. Pour into pre-warmed beer mugs over a silver spoon (to prevent mugs cracking) and serve.

HOT WHISKEY PUNCH

MAKES 1.75L/59.17FL OZ | 20% ALC/VOL | 31.6 STANDARD DRINKS

1L (32fl oz) blended or Irish whiskey

750ml (26fl oz) spring water

1 cup sugar

1 fresh lemon (peeled and sliced)

8 whole cloves

2 cinnamon sticks

Pour water into a saucepan then add sugar, lemon peel, cloves and cinnamon sticks. Bring to the boil, stirring frequently and simmer for 10 minutes. Remove from heat and strain into a clean saucepan. Add whiskey and heat to a simmer without boiling then remove from heat. Pour into coffee glasses over a silver spoon (to prevent glasses cracking) and add a slice of lemon to each serving.

MULLED PORT PUNCH

MAKES 1.25L/42.26FL OZ | 10.5% ALC/VOL | 10.9 STANDARD DRINKS

750ml (26fl oz) tawny port
500ml (17fl oz) spring water
¼ cup sugar
2 fresh oranges (peeled and sliced)
12 whole cloves
cinnamon stick
½ teaspoon allspice (ground)
½ teaspoon mace (ground)
½ teaspoon nutmeg (grated)

Pour water into a saucepan then add sugar, orange peel, cloves, a cinnamon stick, allspice, mace and nutmeg. Bring to the boil stirring frequently to dissolve sugar then simmer for 10 minutes, stirring occasionally. Remove from heat and strain into a small saucepan. Add port and heat to a simmer without boiling whilst stirring occasionally then remove from heat. Pour into coffee glasses over a silver spoon (to prevent glasses cracking) and add a slice of orange to each serving.

WINTER WINE

MAKES 0.47L/15.89FL OZ | 13% ALC/VOL | 5 STANDARD DRINKS

350ml (11⅔fl oz) red wine
60ml (2fl oz) cognac
60ml (2fl oz) spring water
1 tablespoon honey
Pinch of cinnamon
Slices of lemon

Pour wine, cognac, water and honey into a saucepan then add cinnamon. Heat to a simmer without boiling, stirring frequently, then remove from heat and pour into wine glasses over a silver spoon (to prevent glasses cracking). Garnish with a slice of lemon for each serving.

BROWN BETTY

MAKES 2.41L/81.49FL OZ | 9% ALC/VOL | 18 STANDARD DRINKS

1.5L (52fl oz) amber ale
375ml (13fl oz) brandy
540ml (18fl oz) spring water
½ cup brown sugar
1 fresh lemon (sliced)
4 whole cloves
Cinnamon stick
½ teaspoon ginger (ground)
½ teaspoon nutmeg (grated)

Pour water into a saucepan then add sugar, cloves, a cinnamon stick, ginger and nutmeg. Bring to the boil, stirring frequently to dissolve sugar. Simmer for 10 minutes, stirring occasionally, then add ale and brandy. Heat to a simmer without boiling, stirring frequently, then remove from heat and pour into pre-warmed beer mugs over a silver spoon (to prevent mugs cracking). Add a slice of lemon to each serving.

TRINIDAD RUM PUNCH

MAKES 2.65L/89.60FL OZ | 11.1% ALC/VOL | 22.1 STANDARD DRINKS

750ml (26fl oz) dark Trinidad rum
5ml (1/6fl oz) Angostura Bitters
1L (32fl oz) spring water
390ml (13fl oz) fresh lemon or lime juice
500g (1lb 2oz) sugar
Nutmeg

Pour water into a saucepan and add sugar then bring to the boil whilst stirring constantly to dissolve sugar. Add rum, Bitters and juice. Stir and remove from heat. Pour into pre-warmed beer mugs over a silver spoon (to prevent glasses cracking) and sprinkle nutmeg over each serving.

NON-ALCOHOLIC

ANGEL PUNCH

MAKES 5.48L/185.30FL OZ

2L (64fl oz) white grape juice

1.75L (58fl oz) soda water

1L (34fl oz) strong green tea (chilled)

480ml (16fl oz) fresh lemon juice

250ml (8⅓fl oz) sugar syrup

Pour juices, tea and sugar into a chilled punch bowl. Stir well and refrigerate to chill. Add a large block of ice and soda. Stir gently and serve.

CARRY NATION PUNCH

MAKES 3.95L/133.56FL OZ

1.75L (58fl oz) dry ginger ale

1L (32fl oz) fresh orange juice

720ml (24fl oz) fresh lemon juice

240ml (8fl oz) pineapple juice

240ml (8fl oz) sugar syrup

Slices of lemon

Slices of orange

Pour juices and sugar syrup into a chilled punch bowl then stir. Add a large block of ice and ginger ale then stir gently. Add slices of lemon and orange then serve.

GRANNY'S PUNCH

MAKES 3L/101.44FL OZ

750ml (26fl oz) cranberry juice
750ml (26fl oz) pineapple juice
750ml (26fl oz) lemonade
750ml (26fl oz) lemon-lime soda

Pour juices into a punch bowl over a large block of ice and stir. Add lemonade and soda. Stir gently and serve.

7-UP PUNCH

MAKES 3.56L/120.37FL OZ

2L (64fl oz) 7-Up
750ml (26fl oz) fresh orange juice
500ml (17fl oz) spring water
250ml (8⅓fl oz) pineapple juice
60ml (2fl oz) fresh lemon juice
½ cup caster sugar
4 cinnamon sticks

Pour water into a saucepan then add sugar and cinnamon sticks. Heat to a simmer without boiling, stirring occasionally, and allow to simmer for five minutes. Remove from heat and allow to cool to room temperature then refrigerate to chill. Pour into a punch bowl resting on a bed of ice and add juices then stir well. Add 7-Up, stir gently and serve.

BIG PARTY PUNCH

MAKES 6.45L/218.10FL OZ

2.8L (96fl oz) pineapple juice

1.75L (58fl oz) dry ginger ale

820ml (28fl oz) soda water

720ml (24fl oz) fresh orange juice

360ml (12fl oz) fresh lemon juice

2 cups sugar

2 cups strawberries

½ cup fresh mint leaves

Slices of lemon

Slices of orange

Pour juices into a blender without ice and add sugar. Blend well and add mint leaves. Pour into a chilled punch bowl and refrigerate for two hours. Add a large block of ice and ginger ale. Add soda and stir gently. Add strawberries, slices of lemon and orange then serve.

APPLEADE

MAKES 0.60L/20.28FL OZ

600ml (20fl oz) boiling water
½ teaspoon sugar syrup
6 apples (diced)
2 slices of apple

Pour boiling water into a punch bowl over a silver spoon (to prevent glass cracking) and add sugar syrup. Add diced apple and stir well. Allow to stand for ten minutes then strain into a jug and allow to cool. Refrigerate to chill then serve in two collins glasses over ice. Garnish with a slice of apple for each serving.

GLOSSARY

% alc/vol

	% alc/vol	
Ale	5.8	*A type of beer.*
Amaretto	28	*Almond-flavour liqueur that originated in Italy in 1525.*
Angostura Bitters	45	*Produced with infusions of herbs; it is the Bitters that gives pink gin its colour.*
Anisette	30	*Colourless, aniseed-flavour liqueur.*
Applejack	40	*Apple-flavoured brandy produced in America.*
Apricot Brandy	Port	*Apricot-flavoured brandy.*
Apricot Liqueur	23	*Apricot-flavoured liqueur.*
Bacardi	37.5	*Brand name of a light rum produced in Cuba.*
Bailey's Irish Cream	17	*Brand name of a slight chocolate-flavoured Irish cream liqueur produced with a blend of Irish whiskey and cream.*
Banana Liqueur	23	*Banana-flavoured liqueur.*
Beer	5	*Produced from fermentation of cereals and flavoured with hops.*

Bénédictine (D.O.M)	40	Cognac-based sweet herb-flavour liqueur originally created in 1510 by the Benedictine monks, making it one of the world's oldest liqueurs.
Bourbon	40	Sweet whiskey distilled from corn and produced in America.
Brandy	37	Distilled spirit fermented from grapes. If other fruits are used it must be stated on the bottle's label.
Burgundy	11	Red or white wine, mostly still, full-bodied and dry. Originally produced in the Burgundy region of France.
Calvados	40	Apple-flavoured brandy produced in Normandy, France.
Calvert Gin	40	London dry gin produced in America.
Canadian Whisky	38	Delicately flavoured, mild and light-bodied whisky that is produced mainly from corn with proportions of rye, wheat and barley malt.
Champagne	12	Sparkling wine that is produced in the Champagne region of France.
Chartreuse (Yellow)	40	Herbal liqueur produced in France and available in two varieties: yellow—this has a lower alcohol content and green—which has a higher percentage of alcohol per vol at 55% alc/vol.
(Green)	55	
Cherry Brandy	23	Cherry-flavoured brandy.

Cherry Liqueur	*30*	*Cherry-flavoured liqueur.*
Cider	*4.7*	*Fermented apple juice.*
Claret	*11*	*Red table wine.*
Coconut Liqueur	*23*	*Coconut-flavoured liqueur with a light rum-base.*
Coffee Cream Marsala Wine	*15*	*Coffee-flavoured dessert wine.*
Cognac	*40*	*Fine brandy produced in France, no other country is permitted to label their brandy as Cognac.*
Cointreau	*40*	*Sweet orange-flavoured liqueur that is colourless and arguably the world's finest triple sec. It has been produced by the Cointreau family in France since 1849.*
Cranberry Liqueur	*20*	*Cranberry-flavoured liqueur.*
Crème De Cacao	*23*	*Chocolate and vanilla-flavoured liqueur produced from cocoa beans, vanilla and spices. It is available in two varieties: dark and white (clear).*
Crème De Cassis	*20*	*Blackcurrant-flavoured liqueur.*
Crème De Menthe	*23*	*Peppermint-flavoured liqueur produced in three varieties: green, red and white (clear).*

Crème De Noyaux	30	Almond-flavoured liqueur originally produced in France. It is available in two varieties: pink and white (clear).
Curaçao	25	Sweet orange-flavoured liqueur produced from curaçao orange peel. It is available in six varieties: blue, green, orange, red, white (clear) and yellow.
Danish Aquavit	40	Caraway-flavoured Danish aquavit, a pleasant additive in coffee.
Drambuie	40	Scotch whisky-based liqueur flavoured from heather honey and herbs.
Everclear	95	Pure grain alcohol spirit that is also available at 75 per cent alcohol per volume. Alcohol percentage for recipes containing this spirit have been calculated at 95 per cent.
Falernum	11	Low-alcohol liqueur produced from sugar cane and flavoured with almonds, cloves and lime. Originating from Barbados in 1890.
Galliano	35	Aniseed and licorice-flavoured liqueur with a distinctive yellow colour. Produced in Italy from over 80 berries, herbs and roots.
Gin	37	Colourless spirit produced from juniper berries and other botanicals. Grand Marnier gin is the most widely required spirit in cocktails.

Grand Marnier	40	Orange-flavour Cognac-based liqueur produced in France and created in 1880. It is available in two varieties: red ribbon and yellow ribbon—red ribbon has a higher percentage of alcohol per volume 40 per cent.
Green Ginger Wine	14	Jamaican ginger-flavour fruit wine.
Grenadine	Nil	Sweet red syrup, flavoured with pomegranate juice.
Irish Mist	40	Irish whiskey-based liqueur flavoured with herbs and honey.
Italian Brandy	40	Brandy produced in Italy.
Kirsch	37	Clear, bitter cherry-flavoured brandy that can be added to cocktails to enhance the flavour of fruits.
Lambrusco	12	Mellow, sweet red wine to be served chilled.
Leilani Rum	37	Hawaiian rum.
Madeira	12	Fortified wine produced on Madeira Island, Portugal.
Malibu	21	Coconut-flavoured liqueur with a Light Jamaica Rum base. This sweet clear liqueur is produced in Barbados.
Maraschino Liqueur	40	Cherry-flavoured clear liqueur that originated in Italy.

Midori	21	Brand name of a honeydew melon-flavour liqueur that is green in colour and produced by the Suntory Distilling Company in Japan.
Orange Flower Water	Nil	Middle Eastern orange-flavoured water.
Orgeat	Nil	Almond-flavoured syrup.
Peach Brandy	23	Sweet peach-flavoured brandy.
Pernod	40	Aniseed-flavoured liqueur originally produced in France as a substitute for Absinthe.
Pimm's	25	Fruity-bitter liqueur, Pimm's No.1 was created by James Pimm in 1859 in England. Pimm's bases: No.1 Gin, No.2 Whisky, No.3 Brandy, No.4 Rum, No.5 Rye and No.6 is Vodka-based.
Pisang Ambon	21	Banana and herb-flavoured liqueur originating from Indonesia and is produced from the tropical fruits and herbs of South-East Asia.
Port	18	Fortified wine: Ruby—dark and rough, Tawny— smoother and dry and vintage port—this is not a blend and is aged in wooden barrels.
Puerto Rican Rum	38	Clear, dry and light-bodied rum.
Raspberry Liqueur	20	Raspberry-flavoured liqueur.
Rhine Riesling	12	Grape variety, white table wine.

Rosé Wine	12	Crimson-coloured and delicate aroma with the hint of floral scent.
Rosso Antico	17	Fortified red wine aperitif produced from 32 aromatic herbs, produced in Italy.
Rum	37	Spirit distilled from sugar cane syrup, there are many varieties of rum worldwide.
Rum (Dark)	37	Spirit is aged in wooden barrels for between three and 12 years with the addition of caramel added in some cases to darken the spirit. Dark rum varieties include: Jamaica, Haiti and Martinique rums.
Rum (Golden)	37	Spirit aged in charred barrels for three years to produce a golden colour.
Rum (Light)	38	Spirit aged for approximately six to 12 months in oak casks after being distilled in a column-still that produces clear spirit. Originally produced in the southern Caribbean Islands.
Sauterne	12	White table wine produced in the Sauternes region of France.
Schnapps	20	Generic name for flavoured alcohol that is produced from grain or potato mash. Schnapps can be very sweet through to dry with many varieties available. The percentage of alcohol per volume content varies between the varieties. 20% alc/vol is average for commercial schnapps.

Sherry	18	Produced from grapes and fortified with brandy. True Sherry originates from Jerez in southern Spain.
Sloe Gin	26	Sweet gin-based liqueur that is flavoured with sloe plums (blackthorn plums).
Southern Comfort	37	Peach-flavour liqueur that is brandy and bourbon-based. Created by M.W. Heron in New Orleans over 100 years ago.
Spiced Rum	35	Blended with a variety of spices.
Stout	6	Beer that has a strong flavour with a sweet taste.
Strawberry Liqueur	23	Strawberry-flavoured liqueur.
Swedish Punsch	40	Produced from arrack or rum and flavoured with spices, originating from Sweden.
Tequila	38	Spirit distilled from the sap of the dessert dwelling agave plant in Mexico.
Vermouth (Dry)	18	A fortified wine-based apéritif produced from herbs, flowers and roots.
Vermouth (Sweet)	15	
Vodka	37	Clear, odourless and tasteless spirit distilled from fermented grain that has been mashed and filtered through charcoal. Traditional Russian and Polish vodkas have subtle aromas and flavours.

Whiskey 40 *Spirit distilled from grain and then aged. Whiskey is produced in blends and single malts. Irish and rye whiskey is spelt with the 'e', Scotch and Canadian whisky is spelt without.*

INDEX